# DIGGING UP
## THE SALT MINES
*A film memoir*

# SUSANA AIKIN

Digging Up the Salt Mines: A Film Memoir
Copyright 2013 by Susana Aikin

Interior book design by B10 Mediaworx

*To my sons, Ivan and Daniel*

A chilled gust of wind blasted off the river and swept through us like an ice whip. I listened to the kids at my back breathing hard against the cold, and decided it was time to call a formal retreat. Then, suddenly, I saw something move from the corner of my eye. Like seeing a rabbit scamper across a field, swift strokes of a hopping shadow on the edge of the field of vision. I stood very still. It came again across the desolate landscape of abandoned garbage trucks frozen under the pale winter sun. Then the shadow stopped and I saw a slim dark figure emerge by one of the trucks. He was holding a large plastic container in one hand, a large wrench in the other. He was a lean fortyish year old man, wearing a short leather jacket and a faded red bandana around his throat. He just stood there as I approached him, while the kids stayed back and clustered together in a tight shivering knob.

'Miss, he has a weapon,' said Jackie.

He didn't feel threatening to me, just a guy who came from performing some kind of mechanical task, but I still walked towards him cautiously.

'Hey!' I said. 'My name is Susana— How're you doing?'

He nodded shyly. On closer inspection he didn't look threatening at all. His elusive blue eyes had a sadness about them. He had thin yellowish hair and a small mustache. He kept wiping his sniffling nose with his sleeve whenever a gust of wind hit his face.

'We're a high school video team shooting interviews with homeless youth. We were told some might be camping out here. Do you know of anyone?'

He searched my eyes with some hesitation. I felt a bit uncomfortable and confused at what felt like a frisking of my mind. Now, years later, I know that he was looking for signs of trust. But back then I didn't know much about the language and mores of the fringes of society. People living on the edge have their own unique code of trust and honor. It's based on who you are deep down. You can be a murderer yet have a noble heart. You can be apparently kind but have a treacherous soul. I could have been anyone, a disgruntled drug dealer, an undercover policewoman, or anybody else who could bring some degree of harm. This guy was trying to determine what kind of person I was. I was just thinking he might be slightly retarded.

'What's your name?' I asked him.

'Bobby.'

'What do you use that huge wrench for?'

He looked down at the enormous tool in his hand and then seemed to relax. He smiled and said casually, 'Oh, I just use it to get water from the hydrant on the street. We don't have running water here.'

'Oh, who's we? Are there any kids living around here?'

He wavered for a moment.

'Well, not exactly kids. But there's the girls living in the trucks over there'

'Girls! Living in the trucks!'

He looked at me with some embarrassment.

'Would you take me to them? Do you think they'd want to talk to us?'

'Wait a moment,' he said, and I watched him walk towards the back of a mangled truck, its body covered in rust and old graffiti markings.

I turned to the kids.

'Quick, let's set up a camera and sound. It looks like we might be able to interview someone. Come on, no slow motion now. Follow me.'

I t was the fall of 1988 and I had agreed to teach a video class to teenagers at a remedial program for academically failed youth. It proved to be a harder job than I had expected. After a few weeks I was feeling desperate. A dozen teens nodding off through class, snickering at my comments and going into slow motion every time I asked them to do something. I had recently quit a news editor job out of exhaustion and while taking time off to get myself together, I had been offered to teach a video class for Bronx high school drop outs. But soon I was ready to throw in the towel and admit to myself that I just couldn't handle a bunch of unresponsive kids. After all this time I hadn't succeeded in eliciting any interest or sympathy. I could see how they eyed me warily every morning, feeling planets apart from my foreign accent and my downtown looks. But I couldn't back out now. I had to complete the twelve week program I had committed to teach.

The last straw had come the day Norman, the most trying of them all, said to me with that cynical fifty-something look on his cute teen face, 'You know Miss, we're here because we have to be, but we don't give a flying fuck about any of it. All you do is bore us. We don't fall into the trap of thinking we're ever going to work for the networks. So don't try *sooo* hard.'

I stared fixedly into his eyes and he held my gaze in a nonchalant *Idontgiveaflyingfuck* mode without wincing once. After a few seconds of trying to stare him down, I thought, *All right, this actually means I'm not trying hard enough. But if this guy doesn't think I'm as tough as him— I will just have to show him, won't I?*

'Everyone get your coats! Norman, you get the camera and tripod. Tracey, get the sound, James you bring the tapes. Let's go. NOW!'

It was one of those mean November mornings in New York City, the north wind already gathering speed through the tall narrow streets of downtown. I marched them briskly towards the river.

'Where are we going Miss? *It's freezing*', whined one of the girls huddling in her coat while trying to keep up with my military pace. Her thin voice took away some of my steam and I slowed down.

Am I sure about this? I thought suddenly. But the memory of Norman's sneering gaze made me buck up again. No, I need to do this, I'm at the end of my rope here.

We crossed the West Side highway towards the water on Little West 12th Street. The wind blasted us as we stepped out of the claustrophobic urban grid and faced the openness of the river. We stopped for a moment as we reached the other side of the road. The strip was deserted under the leaden sky, only the whizzing of cars and the sharp whistle of the wind could be heard. The group of kids was now gathered around me, disoriented and waiting on my directions. I looked around and then I saw it a few yards away: the enclosed area where the Sanitation Department kept old garbage trucks and the salt for the winter snow. It was a large compound of strange dark buildings surrounded by a wire fence, in the middle of which sat a collection of banged up old trucks. A corrugated metal roof at the entrance protected a huge mountain of grey salt from the wind and the rain I had heard there were homeless teenager hustlers hanging out in there. We were going to seek them out and interview them. I was going to show these kids just how nail tough I could be.

Leaning over the concrete parapet that guarded the sidewalk from the river stood an old grisly man in a beret staring intently into the water. He reminded me of a stranded sailor.

'Do you know if there are any young kids living or working on this side of the river?' I asked him.

He stared shrewdly at me for a moment.

'No kids here. But you have those freaks living there in the trucks. Dirty devils they are. I wouldn't go near them,' he spat in disgust.

'Thank you. Ok guys, let's go!' I said quickly, annoyed at the idea that his words might put off the kids.

But they had already had their effect. I felt an immediate shrinking in the mass of teenage bodies behind me.

A tall girl called Denise said, 'Freaks? Miss, I don't think we need that!'

'Yeah, let's go back and do some writing or somethin,' said James shyly. He was a lanky drooping teen with bad dyslexia.

The others just stared at me in terrified silence, including Norman.

'Guys, we're here, and there's just no sense in going back without anything in the can. So off we go!'

And I started towards the Sanitation Department enclosure. Surprisingly, they followed me meekly like helpless chicks trailing behind the mother hen. As I caught sight of the sinister gray structure a few yards away, I sobered up again.

*Sorry guys,* I thought, *Our fates are sealed. We're crossing this threshold together.*

The whole area of the Sanitation Department bordered the river bank along a stretch of approximately one mile. Its tall wire fence was broken in places and bent in others providing multiple passageways inside the compound. But the main gate was also open and we sailed past a large notice with red letters that read, *Trespassers will be prosecuted.* Inside the enclosure, all was dead except stray pieces of dirty paper and plastic flapping in the cold wind. In fact, the whole place was filled with garbage, as if someone had just scattered the contents of hundreds of garbage bags around.

Very soon we were plodding over bits and pieces of every kind of junk and detritus imaginable inside a trash can. The kids followed behind while I ploughed ahead through the garbage. One girl had pinched her nostrils with her fingers. The stench had already encroached upon us. Had it not been for the chilled wind, it would have been unbearable.

We pushed forward. We passed by the massive grayish mountain of salt under the huge corrugated aluminum roof to our left. I realized this was where Sanitation stored the salt it used to sprinkle on roads and streets when winter snow covered the city. Ahead of us a collection of broken down garbage trucks lay scattered around the enclosure, their dirty white metallic bodies scribbled over with colorful graffiti. At the far end there was what looked like a pier structure sloping towards the water. Supposedly that was the point where the trucks unloaded the garbage onto barges that eventually transported it down the river.

I stopped. There was an eerie silence inside the enclosure. Even the busy highway roaring a few yards away felt muffled from this un-canny point. This suddenly looked like a dead end. How could we find anyone to interview around here?

It was at this moment that Bobby had shown up in the scene.

I walked in the direction that Bobby had gone. A few feet ahead, Bobby stood talking against the graffitied belly of one of the old garbage trucks. For a moment I thought he might be completely mad and put-ting us on. But then I heard a voice coming from the inside of the truck.

'Giovanna, sal del camerino,' It was a deep voice and it spoke in Spanish with a very affected accent. 'Los medios de comunicación nos requieren para una entrevista, Giovanna, come out of the green room. The media is here to interview us.' it drawled, as a disheveled head of reddish fuzzy hair emerged from a narrow vertical opening in one of the truck's mangled doors. She started applying bright red lipstick over her thick lips.

'Hi, I'm Gigi. SO nice to meet you. Where is THAT camera!'

She had an edgy singsong way of speaking, emphasizing certain words very loudly and speaking others quietly. Meanwhile, she was laboriously contorting her body out of the very narrow slit in the truck. First one foot, then another, legs followed and hips wriggled with diffi-culty until finally the whole body was out.

Then she screamed, 'Giovanna! You'll regret it later if you don't come!'

A head of dark curls appeared out of the same crevice and squinted in our direction with a sleepy, ill-humored expression.

'*Que medios! Una blanca con unos niñitos molestando. Yo no salgo! Y además que frio hace!!!* What media! A white girl with a bunch of kids coming to bother us. I am not going out! And it's sooo cold!!' she said wrapping her collar tight around her neck.

We were all dumbstruck. They were not kids, they were not girls, nor were they men. They were men dressed as women. But not just men dressed as women, they were – I guess the word is transvestites, but that is not what entered my mind. At that moment I was just struck by their hybrid beauty. They looked like feminized men or masculinized women. Something in between both sexes. Something separate from men and women, but still belonging both. They had slim hips and feminine lips, big hands and feet and almond eyes. They had long hair and lipstick, earrings and nail polish. And, women's colorful ragged clothes and other tattered pieces of attire. And they were sleeping inside the belly of garbage trucks. They looked like faded pretty dolls who had been long stuck inside a trash can.

Giovanna started backing into the truck when I stepped forward. '*Si, hace mucho frio. Les traemos un café si quieren,*' I spoke in Spanish, my native language. I offered to bring them coffee. It was the magical key that opened the door.

Giovanna spun around, her eyes lit up, '*Hablas español!*' she was surprised I spoke Spanish and thrilled about the idea of hot coffee.

'Are we really going to be on TV? OH, MY GAAAD!' pealed Gigi and forced herself back into the truck to prepare for the occasion.

I turned around and gave two of the kids some money to bring coffee.

'Everyone else stay on the job. This is happening.' I ordered.

We all got busy setting up the camera and sound equipment.

The coffee arrived sooner than expected and taking two steaming cups over to the truck, I talked to them through its metal surface.

'Hey, coffee is here!'

Gigi and Giovanna emerged once more from the opening in the truck. This time not only laboriously but with extreme care, since now they were supposedly dressed to the nines. They wore dirty jeans and sweaters. Gigi had on a short black leather jacket and Giovanna wore a torn long red leather coat. They wore pink and green scarves and bandanas draped around their necks. Giovanna was also wearing a dark green velour headband. They moved with extreme affectation as though they were great actresses walking the red carpet or famous models on the catwalk. Once out of the belly of the truck they climbed onto the hood of the vehicle and arranged themselves in sprawling positions. They were putting on a real act for us. They reminded me of those ads from the fifties with beautiful models stretched out over lustrous cars.

'Ok, we're ready. Shoot!'

I turned to Norman and for the first time saw a glint of engrossment on his face.

'Ready? Roll camera!' I started, 'Tell us why you're here'

A flood of information followed, as they both poured out their stories, overlapping and intertwining their accounts, while sipping their coffee in ladylike fashion.

They told us they were homeless crack addicts who worked as prostitutes at night in the nearby Meatpacking District and then crashed inside the garbage trucks during the day. In the summer they had all lived on top of the salt mountain under the shed, but it had become impossible when the cold set in and they moved inside the trucks. The street name for this place was *The Salt Mines* and they were called the *Salt People*. Most of them where Latino: Gigi was from Puerto Rico and Giovanna from Dominican Republic, and there were others from the Bronx and East Harlem.

'I'm here because I lost my apartment and my lover got arrested and sent to Rikers Island,' said Gigi pursing her lips.

'I'm just a girl down on her luck,' laughed Giovanna.

'We're a family of Latin queens,' drawled Gigi

'What about Bobby?' I asked.

'Oh, he's not with us. He's independent,' said Gigi.

'But sometimes when he's lonely he comes to visit,' added Giovanna with a malicious smile.

'So, who's Gigi and who's Giovanna? I'm kind of confused with all these names beginning with G,' I said.

They laughed. 'Drag queens just looooove Gs—G strings, G spots, sexy Italian names starting with G…'

'No really, I'm Gigi, the red head from Puerto Rico.'

'And I'm Giovanna, the dark brunette from the Dominican Republic—mind you, raised in the Bronx.'

*Am I ever going to remember these differences,* I mused. But I only said, 'It's so nice to meet you Gigi from PR and Giovanna from Dominican.'

They smiled back contentedly.

It was getting late and the wind was picking up speed over the water and sweeping through *The Salt Mines* like a razor blade. For a moment I came out of my trance and realized everyone around me was shivering. The effects of the caffeine were waning and the sun was diving fast into a blaze of deep crimson smeared over the horizon.

'What else do you want to know?'

Gigi's eyes and nose were watering from the cold.

'Can I come another day?' I asked.

'Sure, you can come anytime. *The Salt Mines* is open to everyone. We're the only open condo in New York City. You can even move in with us,' Giovanna said with a deep hoarse laugh that died into a groan.

'It's so cold and I am soo hungry,' she said turning to Gigi.

She suddenly looked like a man. Her makeup had faded and her lips looked pale and taut.

We returned to the school building in silence. The experience had been too intense to even begin to talk about it. The kids put away the equipment and left for the day. I went home. My partner Carlos, who was a freelance cameraman, was in Florida shooting a news documentary and wouldn't return to the city for a couple of days. So, I spent the rest of the day by myself in the apartment. I couldn't do anything. I couldn't read or write or even talk on the phone. My head was swimming with images from the world I had entered into that afternoon. The experience had totally yanked me out of my snug paradigm. I had never imagined there could be people living inside garbage trucks. The image of Gigi squiggling out of the slit belly of the truck kept playing itself over and over in my mind like a broken record. The vulnerability of their eyes behind the heavy makeup, the openness and simplicity with which they shared their stories, had pierced my heart. Images of the garbage, the dirty gray salt, the grotesqueness of it all, swirled in my dreams all night. By next morning, I understood that *The Salt Mines* had blasted my brain. And that my life would never be the same again.

The next day when I went back to Educational Video Center, Steve, the director of the program for drop out youths, had already looked at the footage I shot with the kids.

'It's great you're taking the kids around the city and shooting on the street. But I don't think you should take them back to places like these. I want you to start working with them on a documentary about AIDS with kids their age, kids similar to them, so they realize how close they can be to it.'

I tried to argue, but Steve was not one to be easily dissuaded from his ideas or purposes. I couldn't take the kids down to *The Salt Mines* anymore. When I got together with the kids again in class, I asked them if they had any interest in going back to shoot in *The Salt Mines*, but I only got sluggish reactions. Not one of them was interested in going back.

However, all that didn't matter anymore. I had already made up my mind that the story inside that enclosure merited a real documentary, not just a piece shot by kids for a class. The footage we had gotten that day was great, if you put aside the gondola style camera work, and the parts where the sound in the interviews suddenly died. It was only good for studying the subjects and planning future shoots.

It was also good for enticing Carlos into the project. When he got back from his shoot, I showed him the footage. I literally saw his jaw drop.

'Holy Cow, this is unbelievable! Totally surreal!'

'Don't you think it could be a cool story to shoot?'

'I think it's an amazing story.'

'Do you want to shoot it together?'

'Sure!'

I was dying to shoot a documentary. I had moved to New York City six years before with the objective of becoming a filmmaker. With no money to go to film school, I had strived to learn the trade through workshops, internships and volunteer work on independent productions, student films and low budget commercials, while surviving on waitressing and low paying clerical jobs in the meantime. Now the time was ripe for me to leap into my first large project. I was ready to get into an independent production of our own, prepared to put every resource and penny I had into a real documentary. A few months before, Carlos and I had shot a short video together before, a piece called *Pier 34*, which explored a dilapidated pier on the Hudson that had become an underground gallery for artists to create striking murals depicting the brutality and darkness of the Reagan years. *Pier 34* had whet my appetite for filming larger projects. That appetite had turned into insatiable hunger once I entered the world of *The Salt Mines*.

Images were my passion. When I first arrived in New York, I bought myself a Super 8 camera with my first paycheck and would shoot around the city whenever I was off work. Back in my room, I would play the images over and over in a small Moviola I had set up next to my bed, an old fashion editing device with a small screen and two lateral cranks to manually move the film strips back and forth for viewing.

I had been brought up learning poetry. In my family, the children were made to learn long poems by heart and then asked to recite them in front of guests and friends. I had learnt early on that poetry had the power of evoking images in the mind. The poems I loved told stories by bringing up striking images strangely juxtaposed with one another. Later, the mere sounds of the words could bring forth those images again whenever recited or just held long enough in the conscious mind. Now I had taken a step forward in the direction of understanding poetics through images. Watching movement emerge frame by frame on the screen, watching colors change in depth and texture through the variations of light, was a riveting experience that filled me with emotion. Some images could stay with me for weeks or even months as if they had been etched on my brain. It could be anything, the expression of a face, the swaying branches of a tree in the wind, the city glittering in the dusk from a roof top. Powerful images could also spontaneously leap out of my memory at any given moment and pour back into my consciousness, eliciting the original emotion all over again. Images of beauty, startling or disquieting images could possess me over and over again, throwing me into elated or agitated states of mind. I started looking at photographs and films with a different eye, even with caution. I knew how deeply they could affect me, how they had the capacity of moving me at a cellular level. I started understanding how images could move multitudes, deeply influence opinions and behavior, even change the course of history.

Now, I wanted to use this power to tell stories to the world.

I had met Carlos while taking a video workshop at Downtown Community Television Center, a media center located in an old firehouse in Lafayette Street. DCTV was then a hip, friendly media center swarming with the wildest assortment of wannabes film and video makers from all parts of the country and walks of life. In order to rent their low cost video equipment it was first necessary to take a production workshop that would ensure you knew how to handle it properly. Carlos was the instructor of the workshop I took and, realizing we were both from Spain, we got talking after class. Carlos had just returned from

Nicaragua where he had been spending time reporting on the Contra War while traveling in the jungle with Sandinista troops. At the time the US government was secretly funding a counterrevolutionary war against the Sandinistas about which there was fast growing opposition among US citizens. A number of independent journalists and reporters traveled down to Nicaragua to report on the situation. Carlos was one of them.

We sat at the counter of a Dunkin' Donuts near DCTV and ordered coffee. He told me stories of disjointed troops of young soldiers armed with old rifles who were made to march for days through the jungle with hardly any food or camping gear. There had been a few attacks on some of the units he traveled with and he had witnessed military action first hand. Once, he told me, he had stayed up all night with a soldier who had been mortally wounded during a Contra assault, until he died at dawn. There were no medical supplies to help him with. Not even painkillers. He was only nineteen years old.

Carlos had slept in hammocks hung from trees in the rain forest and eaten armadillo meat when there was nothing else around. He had endured weeks of incessant mosquito bites and constant assailing by a species of tiny red ticks that the soldiers spent hours on end removing from one another. In the pictures I later saw, he is in a group of soldiers all in shabby fatigue gear and armed with an assortment of pistols and ancient looking rifles. He alone stands in the middle with a Nikon camera. I had never met anyone who had been in a war or even traveled by foot in the jungle. I came from a middle-class family, and ended up a renegade law student who had escaped to New York to become a filmmaker. I was fascinated by his stories.

I didn't see him again for two years. Then, I called him to ask him for a recommendation letter for my application to NYU film school. By that time he had set up a small video production company with an colleague and was working as a freelance cameraman. I didn't get into NYU, but I got together with Carlos. A few months later we moved into a tiny one bedroom apartment in Chelsea. Immediately, we set about making films together.

At that time, New York seemed to me a two-faced city. On the one hand there was the glittering facade of its skyline, with majestic mid-town high rises, busy multibillion-dollar businesses, mazes of the fanciest shops in the world, and hordes of fast paced go-getters. And then, there was the darker face, the broken down neighborhoods some of which felt like post-war zones, the dirty streets with piles of uncollected garbage and graffiti scribbled all over ruinous buildings with hundreds of homeless men in tatters pushing old supermarket carts, huddling on street corners or sleeping on park benches.

The Reagan administration had been drastically cutting social spending on subsidized housing, closing down mental hospitals and throwing thousands of people out on the streets in the process, most of them disabled or mentally challenged. Although the Bowery had long been a refuge for hobos and alcoholics, walking down its dreary avenue towards DCTV in the late '80s was a heartbreaking experience, with its ever changing crowd of ruddy faced men with glazed eyes hanging out day and night totally slammed, a collection of old winos who slept on pavements and lined up in soup kitchens along the streets. At night they stood warming up around fires they would make inside large metal garbage cans. The Bowery was famous for its line of fires burning like torches and lighting the way in the cold winter nights. The police must have swept them away every few days, because there always seemed to be a different crowd. Different faces, but with the same old dirty clothes, same bottles in their hands, same slurred speech and staggering gait.

It wasn't only the Bowery; the whole city seemed to invaded by swarms of homeless people. One time, I was strolling through the East Village at night with a friend who was visiting from out of town. Small cafes and shops sparkled along the way with colored lights inside their mysterious little doors. The East Village was the hip hangout of the day, where artists, community activists and visionaries met. It started to snow. As we hurried along the narrow streets toward the subway we came upon a huge rolled carpet laid across on the pavement. When our turn came to cross it, a woman who had just jumped over it said, 'Don't step on it. There's a guy inside.'

I looked at her in utter disbelief and I was about to take it all as a joke, when I heard a voice coming from inside the carpet.

'No, really, it's okay. When people step on me, it warms me up.'

I looked down horrified.

'Only in New York,' commented my friend with an uneasy laugh.

But the comment hurt. I felt totally helpless and pained by this unbearable side of the city I had come to love passionately. Something in me was screaming to blast these images out into the world.

Carlos and I worked for Television of Spain on Madison Avenue for a couple of years. He was a director cameraman and I worked as a news editor. It was an intense job, although fairly lucrative because at the time news bureaus paid well. But the editing was extremely demanding, since news slots had to be fed daily very early, in order to get over to Europe by their evening news time. The camera crew would come back to the office around 11 am and a three to five minute segment would have to be ready for the feed at noon, since given the six hour difference with Spain, that is when it would reach their evening news program in time. The pressure to edit fast and dirty was excruciating. Specially for me, who had been trained to dwell on beautiful seamless cuts and meaningful messages. This pressure was aggravated by the politics inside the news agency. Huge egos, malicious competition, bad mouthing and back stabbing were rampant. And reporters and senior news producers were always political choices sent from Spain, so there were no opportunities to move up. At one point we both got fed up and quit. Carlos also ended his relationship with his business partner and quit the production company shortly after.

Suddenly, we were both jobless. But we had some equipment. Carlos had obtained a Betacam camera, a couple of microphones, a tripod and a reel-to-reel editing system from the dissolution of his company. This might seem trifling today because video equipment is so inexpensive. But back then video equipment was exclusively expensive, and not the cute little techie objects of the present day, but big bulky, heavy metallic pieces, difficult to carry and store. Nevertheless, I was elated. We could start our own production company and make our own films. Of course, we would be moonlighting in the process to pay the bills.

Our Chelsea apartment had one big walk in closet with a small window that the landlord had called a second bedroom, but frankly, it could hardly hold the length of a mattress. It became our equipment storage room and our crammed editing room. Now we needed a name, a worthy label under which to work.

We took off to Maine for a long weekend in order to rethink our lives. Driving up the coastal roads in a rented car, we pulled off to find wooden cabins for the night along the shore. We bought fresh lobster in local fish markets and feasted on them back in the cabin, sleeping afterwards in each other's arms on floor rugs besides blazing fireplaces. It was late October and the vacation season was over. The coast was deserted of visitors and tourists, only local fishermen and townspeople could be seen occasionally going about their business. In the afternoons the light was golden over the cobalt sea. The air smelt of salt and iodine sprayed from the cold waves lashing and breaking over the rocky coast. One day we walked on a dark rocky platform at the end of a long strip of beach. The porous rock was full of tiny pools swarming with crabs, barnacles and swishing algae. A few feet ahead, a myriad splashes of orange and yellow glistened on the dark surface of the reef. As I drew near, I was surprised to see hundreds of starfish basking in the late afternoon light. They were all sizes, from massive to tiny, a huge tribe of these mysterious five-footed creatures that I only knew as lonely inhabitants of deep sea waters. The vision was magical. It spoke of the boundless abundance of the sea. It struck me as a symbol of endless creative possibilities.

I said to Carlos, 'Let's call our company Starfish Productions.'

He looked at me for a moment and then at the starfish.

'Not bad,' he mused and then after a beat, 'Okay. Agreed.'

He took out his Nikon camera and started taking pictures of the starfish. I picked up the largest I could find and put it over my head as if it were an exotic hat.

'Take a picture of me. It can be our logo'

'Umm, I'm not sure how marketable it would be for a serious company,' he said laughing while he took a bunch of pictures.

Days later back in New York City I asked a designer friend to create a logo for our new company. He produced a beautiful white silhouetted starfish shape against a dark blue background. We had a logo. We were ready to start.

To my frustration, we couldn't return to *The Salt Mines* until the day after Thanksgiving. We just couldn't get out of our Thanksgiving compromise with some very dear friends. I would have rather gone back to the trucks and started filming again, I was so obsessed with my experience, but I just had to wait it out. For the first time since I was in the United States I accepted massive amounts of leftovers from our friends' very generous table. I knew where I was going to take them.

Finally, the day after Thanksgiving Carlos and I went down to *The Salt Mines* together. This time we took our professional camera and sound equipment. We arrived in the early afternoon. It was even colder than the last time. The taxi left us on the narrow sidewalk near the gate. We lugged the camera equipment to the entrance of the Salt Mine. I left Carlos guarding the equipment while I went scouting inside the enclosure. It was as spectral as I remembered it. I found it difficult to identify the one truck from which I had seen Gigi and Giovanna emerge, since all the trucks looked similar, their bodies all banged up and covered in graffiti scrawlings. I went up to a couple of them and knocked and called out their names but there was no response. I walked around, or more, I waded through garbage for a while but the place seemed deserted.

I returned to the gate in a state of utter frustrated.

'What took you? It's freezing. Did you find anyone?' asked Carlos.

I was about to say no, but as I looked ahead I saw a group of people leaning against the parapet close to the pier by the river.

'There they are! Quick, let's go.'

We grabbed the equipment and made for the pier. As we approached I saw there were about ten of them huddling in their coats and talking in small groups. The wind seemed to hit harder at that point than any other, and for a moment I stood trying to figure out why they would be standing there instead of taking refuge inside the compound or the trucks. Most of them were very poorly dressed with just jackets or thin coats and some wore skirts with no tights or socks.

I recognized Gigi and walked up to her calling her name.

'Gigi, we brought food from last night's Thanksgiving dinner,' and I handed her the bags of delicious leftovers.

'Oh, here you are! You said you were coming days ago. We were waiting. There is somebody who wants to meet you,' she made a gesture towards the water. And as I looked I saw a slender figure with shoulder length blond hair talking animatedly with two others while holding tight to her tattered camel coat.

'SARA!' screamed Gigi, 'Here's the woman who wants to make a movie!'

Sara whipped her head in my direction and we locked eyes for a split second. She had a beautiful face with delicate features, a small nose, high cheeks and well delineated lips. Inside her almond shaped eyes burned a fierce torch, a determination I had never seen before. She made a beeline for me.

'So, you are Susana! The filmmaker from Spain. And can you guess WHY my name is Sara?' She turned her face to the side so I could see her profile. 'Because everyone says I look EXACTLY like Sara Montiel,' she added pushing her nose higher up in the air. 'Don't you think so?'

I looked at her and yes, actually she did look like Sara Montiel, a well-known Spanish actress of my parents' generation who had been considered a real beauty in her day. Her legend as the sex symbol of her time had pervaded in Spain and Latin America throughout the decades.

'You definitively *do* look like her!' I said.

Sara beamed at me. 'THANK YOU! You are also EXTREMELY beautiful. And WHO is this?'

She batted her eyelids at Carlos with a look of utter awe on her face.

'Oh, this is Carlos. He's my partner. We work together.'

'Do you work the bedroom together as well as the camera?' she asked, still looking at him totally mesmerized.

'Actually we do,' I said, blushing slightly.

'I thought so!' she said and then turning to me, 'Tell me about your film.'

All the others were now sitting or leaning on the concrete parapet and wolfing down the Thanksgiving leftovers. Turkey sandwiches, sweet potatoes, pumpkin pie, the whole lot. They ate coarsely and hungrily as if they hadn't eaten in weeks. Two of them were having a discussion and started throwing food savagely at each other while they screamed and pealed with laughter. Sara held a turkey sandwich daintily with her fingers, and nibbled at it with exaggerated minuscule bites. It was like a grotesque theater scene.

'I want to film you. I want to know everything about your lives, how come you ended up living in this place. I want to know how dressing like a woman feels like – everything.'

'All right, I accept. When do we start?' she said immediately.

'Right now,' I said and I turned around looking for Carlos. But he was already filming the group interacting over the food.

The roar of an approaching engine suddenly broke into the scene and I saw a huge gray four wheeler parking a few yards away. Another vehicle followed. All at once the transvestites threw down everything they had in their hands and started running towards the two cars. I looked at Sara in confusion.

'Our meeting is over. I have to run now,' she said, getting ready to bolt.

'What's going on?' I asked

'Never mind. I'll tell you later.' She was already disappearing into one of the vehicles.

'When should I come again?'

But the cars where already whizzing out of the drive into the highway. On the back of the last car pulling out I caught sight of a bumper sticker: 'JESUS SAVES'.

W e started going down to *The Salt Mines* every day we were off work. We lived on 21st Street, so we weren't that far away, although we had to take a taxi each time because of the heavy equipment we were carrying. The days were short since it was close to the winter solstice, so we had to reach the place early in the day before the sun went down. However we couldn't get there too early, in fact definitely not before noon, because the Salt people had probably been working the street most of the night and they would be sleeping in the trucks. But we soon learnt that there was no regular schedule in *The Salt Mines*, no regular population, no regular habits. Every day was a completely new reality. Some people stayed for a few days, others for a few hours, others just when they couldn't find any other place to go. Only the most desperate made it some kind of a home. Those whose crack addiction had totally disconnected them from mainstream reality. So going into *The Salt Mines* was each time an unpredictable and drastically different adventure.

The next time we went in search of Sara after meeting her by the river was a Saturday early in the afternoon. At the time I didn't know that Saturdays were the worst days to catch any of them in the trucks because Friday night was the best night of the week when it came to working the street. If you had any appeal and craft as a transvestite, you were likely to hook up with enough clients to make you a pile of money and end up in a hotel room with a generous trick.

It had been drizzling all morning so the ground inside *The Salt Mines* was drenched and the whole crust of garbage on the ground had become a soggy glob that squished up and down under my feet. I had left Carlos close to the salt mountain under the aluminum roof so that the equipment wouldn't get wet if it started to rain again. I searched the whole compound, timidly at first, and later calling their names out loud. But there was no response. The place was a silent wasteland.

I was beginning to feel desperate when I saw a tall black man covered in dark garbage bags pushing an old supermarket cart overloaded with all sorts of objects, from suitcases and broken down appliances to plastic bags full of bottles and cans.

'Excuse me — Hello!'

He ignored me and continued plowing through the garbage. When I caught up with him, I was surprised to see that a large part of his cart filled with a collection of old books. Books on economics, politics and social theory. I even caught glimpse of a shabby hardcover version of Adam Smith's *The Wealth of Nations*.

'Hello. Sir?'

He must have been in his late forties. He had fine features, high cheek bones and deep ebony eyes.

'Excuse me, I am looking for a group of people who are staying here. In the trucks. Have you seen anybody?'

'What do you want with them?' His voice had a strong African accent.

'I'm doing a documentary about homelessness and I want to interview them'

'Hmm.'

The more I looked at him the more I saw a majestic element about him, the way he carried his body in a very erect position, the way he had organized the stuff in the cart, even in the way he wore black bags over his clothes and around his head, turban style, as a shield against the wind.

'Do you also live here?'

'I don't live anywhere in particular!' he snapped, and I cringed at the thought that I might have offended him.

'Sorry, I just meant if you..'

'I only come here looking for objects and books,' he said more calmly.

'What do you do with the books?' I asked

'I study them.' he answered and then after a beat, 'You look surprised. Do you think all homeless people are poor, ignorant or just stupid?'

'I don't think that,' I started to say feeling embarrassed and confused.

'I was a university professor in my country before I came to America. I lectured on Economics.'

'What country are you from?'

'Senegal. Do you even know where it is?' he sneered.

I nodded and saw something yield in his expression.

'So, what happened? Why are you now on the streets?' I mumbled in disbelief.

'It became harder and harder to pay my rent until one day I decided it wasn't worth it to spend my life making money to pay bills. I didn't want to give all my blood to the capitalist system. It was better to lose my apartment and spend my time reading and writing my book.'

I looked at him in amazement.

'Would you tell me all this on camera? Can I interview you about your experience?'

He stared fixedly at the ground.

'No, it wouldn't make a difference. People don't care. It's a waste of time. Believe me, you're wasting your time.'

'But it's just that people don't know that these things are happening, they need to be told, it's the only way we can change things…' I protested passionately.

'Nothing can change the world. No, I won't tell my story,' he said as he started pushing the cart away, 'And besides, you know, us Africans don't believe in cameras. We think they steal away parts of our souls'

'Come on, you're a professor. You don't believe that, do you?' I walked after him but he didn't stop.

'It doesn't matter. I'm still African.' his last words were trailed by the wind. In a moment he was gone from sight.

When I got back to Carlos and told him about the encounter, he said 'Don't get frustrated. It might be like this many times. You're going to have to develop some patience if you want to work with homeless people.'

I couldn't believe how cool and detached this guy could be. One of his sound recording colleagues always called him the Zen Cameraman. I was the total opposite: emotional, insecure, and reactive to the smallest detail. A producer in the making with a lot to learn.

The next day we went down to *The Salt Mines* we met Little Man for the first time.

'They call me Little Man 'cause I'm short. But I'm strong. And I have a brain too,' he said pointing at his left temple. He was wearing a dirty woolen cap pulled down to his ears. His black eyes were sharp but the rest of his face was pulled into a permanent grin. He had a small wiry body that was in constant motion. He bounced up and down and skipped more than he walked. At the time I thought it might have to do with the cold, that he was just jumping around to warm up. But later I understood it had to do with his nervous system and his drug use. Gigi told us later that he was always restless and could get really violent when he smoked crack.

We told him we were filming a documentary and asked him if he would like to talk about his experience on camera.

'Naah, I've nothing to tell. I'm only here for a short while.'

Then Carlos asked him if he would show us around.

'OK,' he said jumping backwards as Carlos followed him with the camera.

When he got to the salt mountain he said, 'This is the Salt Mine. We used to live here. No more. Now we live in the trucks.' He ran nimbly up the salt slope and when he reached the top, rolled back down and somersaulted, landing in front of the camera like an acrobat.

'We're OK. We're all together. We have some fights and shit. But we survive. That's the name of the game,' he concluded looking intently at the camera while pointing his index finger at the sky.

Little Man took us around the enclosure. He showed us where he stored the woodpile he collected from the garbage to make fire with. Then he pointed to an abandoned toilet standing between two of the trucks, hopped over and sat down on the toilet seat.

He flashed a crooked smile at the camera and said, 'See, even our little toilet here…' Then he jumped up again and disappeared behind a truck. We picked up the camera and tried to follow him, but he was nowhere to be seen.

As we walked around trying to follow Little Man I realized this place was a maze, one narrow corridor between trucks the same as the next, with identical and indistinguishable pieces of garbage on the ground, and the same indifferent strips of sky above our heads. I was beginning to see the Salt Mine as the symbol of a certain kind of prison, a pocket of hell outside of which it was impossible to climb out. A dumping ground for disposable beings.

When it became obvious that we wouldn't find Little Man, we considered leaving for the day after taking some random shots of the enclosure. Close ups of what might have been a dazzling white stiletto shoe standing alone on one of the trucks, a Raggedy Ann doll peeking out of a conglomerate blob of debris, the front of one of the trucks where someone had painted sad eyes around the head lights.

But suddenly, a few feet ahead of us, we spotted Gigi combing her hair in front of a truck wing mirror.

'Hey! Where's everyone?'

'I'm the only one around today. I don't know where the others are. They might have been arrested last night or found a fat trick.'

'Gigi, will you talk to us on camera?'

'Sure, what do you want to know?' She turned back to the mirror for a second and checked her face and nose. She was wearing traces of black eye pencil around her eyes and was dressed in faded jeans with a short leather jacket. Her oval face was framed by shoulder length red hair cut in layers. Her skin was light bronze with sprinkled acne scars around the cheeks. She had an aquiline nose and curvy lips, prone to pouting. Her brown eyes were deep with a fierce sadness.

'Tell us everything about *The Salt Mines*,' I said.

She swept her gaze around and smiled coyly.

'What is there to say? We lived on top of the salt mine over there in the summer and it was a riot. Imagine all kinds of drag queens hanging out and creating all sorts of scandal. It got to be so fun that even a bunch of queens who were not homeless came to stay with us. TV reporters interviewed us, even people from the radio. It was a glorious time. Then the cold came and everyone disappeared. The few that were left had to move into the trucks. It wasn't fun anymore. But what can we do? We're steeped in vice'

'Can you show us where you live?'

Gigi led the way towards one of the trucks. She moved slowly and rigidly. I wondered whether it was her personal way to fend off the cold.

'This is my home right now,' she said with a smirk and pointed towards a gnarled opening on the metal surface of the truck she was standing next to.

'Can you get back in there and show us from the inside?'

She started twisting and turning her body to fit in through the narrow opening. When she had disappeared into the truck, Carlos turned on the Sun Gun – a sort of flash light on top of the camera— and approached the dark orifice. The light blasted into the darkness revealing an old dirty mattress covered in bundles of clothes and plastic bags. Gigi was lying on top of it all.

'This is my home. You can see my mattress here, my stuff…'

'Do you live here alone?'

'Most days I have a girlfriend staying over. If Edwin's in town he always stays with me. Then it's definitely a *Don't Disturb* situation!' she laughed.

'Who's Edwin?'

'Edwin is my lover. He's in prison right now. But he'll be out soon'.

'And how come you ended living in a place like this?'

'Edwin and I came from Puerto Rico to the U.S. hoping to get off to a new start. But then crack showed up and everything went to hell.'

I didn't know anything about crack at the time, nothing beyond the fact that it was a very addictive derivative of cocaine that was fast becoming popular in the city. Small opaque vials were increasingly found scattered around in streets and parks, and stories about extreme violence and aggression in users filled the local news. But this was a new face of crack for me. Addiction to the point of homelessness inside a garbage dump, prostitution to acquire, or even just to smoke the drug with the trick.

Night was rapidly descending over *The Salt Mines*.

'I think I'll go over to the meat market and meet some friends,' Gigi said 'Of course, I need to get ready first,' she laughed coyly and seeing I didn't quite understand what she meant, hurried to explain, 'You know, I need to put on some lipstick and stuff.'

'Can we film you doing that?' I asked her tentatively.

I wasn't sure what our boundaries were in terms of filming. I felt too shy to make requests. I hadn't yet developed the pushy persona of a full-blown producer. But Gigi was very flattered by my request. In fact she probably talked about *getting ready* on purpose, so we would film. As I would soon learn, the moment of putting on clothes and makeup is a sacred ritual for a drag queen, the ceremonial bridge that enables the crossing between gender worlds.

Gigi disappeared for a few moments and came back with a bag. She placed it on the front surface of the nearest truck and proceeded to take out its contents. Compact powder, foundation, eyeliner, a very complete cosmetic set in all. Finally, she leaned a magnifying mirror against the truck window. Carlos switched on the Sun Gun and Gigi smiled nervously under the harsh light.

'We're on,' Carlos already had his eye in the viewfinder.

Gigi started applying makeup in front of the mirror. She applied foundation all over her face with special emphasis on her acne speckled cheeks, then delineated the contours of her eyes with dark blue eye liner and softly brushed pink blush on her cheeks. I watched in fascination as she dabbed her pouting lips with deep red lipstick. She worked quickly with extreme concentration. Then she took a hairbrush from the bag and brushed her dark red hair vigorously, first with her head bent over and afterwards with her head tilted backwards. When she was done she turned and looked at us. Her transformation was complete. Her features were strongly enhanced, particularly her eyes. They reminded me of the eyes of Egyptian statues, thickly traced in navy blue lines.

We heard steps shuffling towards us. A round face with shiny black eyes and soft lips stepped into the ring of light that shone off the Sun Gun.

'Oh, this is my friend Jenny,' said Gigi, but didn't bother to introduce us to her.

Jenny looked at us shyly and without any questions about the filming, joined the scene and started talking to Gigi as if we weren't there. We took it as a gesture of consent to be part of the scene and kept on shooting. She was a short curvy transvestite. Her thick knees and calves shone in the light under her very short mini skirt, and she wore black pumps so tight over her wide feet, that they looked as if they were going to burst. Seeing Gigi doing finishing touches on her makeup, she also approached the mirror and extracting a bar of lipstick out of her tiny book bag, applied it to her lips.

'Does my makeup look good?' asked Gigi turning towards her. Jenny nodded as if it were an annoying question.

After a beat, Gigi said, 'Hey, can I borrow a condom?' her tone now sounded more like a pleading. 'I'm penniless and I need a condom to work the first trick.'

Jenny hesitated for a moment, her eyes darting between the camera and Gigi. She might have been trying to figure out how much information Gigi was giving us about their lifestyle.

'Sorry, but I have only one left,' she said after a beat, 'That way I can do my own trick, get some cash and then buy more,' and she stared at the camera looking for approval.

Suddenly I had the feeling they were putting on a scene for us, a sort of theatrical skit revealing of the responsible attitude of street hustlers towards the public spread of AIDS or other sexually transmitted diseases. I let go of the thought and didn't say anything. We were filming this scene without any interference, *fly-on-the-wall* style.

They stood for a moment in silence, then Gigi said, 'I think I'll have an early night today. I got to bed real late yesterday.'

'I had a great night yesterday. I made lots of money,' Jenny had a slight lisp in which she rolled her r's and s's.

'I made more than $200,' retorted Gigi.

'I made over $300,' said Jenny.

They started a contest about who had made the most the night before. To the money, they started adding the amounts of crack that had been given them by dealers and tricks. This obviously counted as some kind of qualified currency. I wondered again if this was all true or just an act for the camera, since the quantities kept building up as they spoke. It might have been that Gigi was bragging in front of the camera and needed to end up with the highest amount of gain for the record. But

Jenny was proving to be a tough adversary. Finally, Gigi seemed to have had enough.

'Okay, I'll see you later in the street,' she said and this sounded like the code indicating that Jenny needed to leave. This was Gigi's gig alone. Jenny seemed to hesitate for a beat, then set her stuffed feet in motion and tottered away into the darkness.

G igi obviously hadn't had enough of the camera.

'We can go sit over there,' she said pointing out into the indistinct darkness, 'There's a few crates. It's what you might call our living room here in the Mines,' she added with a raspy laugh.

Carlos directed the Sun Gun in the direction she was pointing. It was a wide opening between the rows of trucks. Our eyes followed as the strobing camera light searched blinkingly over a collection of crates, a few broken chairs and stools standing in a circle around one strange center piece. It was a yellow or dirty golden couch cut like a fat triangle, what might have the corner piece of a large L-shaped sofa in its heyday. It stood tilted to one side because of a missing leg. In the middle of the circle before it was a bundle of burnt sticks covered in ashes.

A bonfire! I hadn't quite believed Little Man earlier when he had talked about having a regular provision of wood for making fires. I felt an immense relief at the idea of starting a fire since I was very cold and tired, but Gigi just sat on one of the crates with no apparent intention of doing anything else.

'Please,' she waved her hand indicating us to sit around her, 'This is where we receive our visitors,' she added jokingly.

'Can we light a fire?' I asked.

'Oh, sure!' she said and, getting up, walked a few feet away and came back shortly with a bundle of sticks and pieces of wood in her arms. She placed them over the ashes and inserted pieces of carton and paper underneath. She felt her pockets for a lighter and started igniting the carton and blowing softly into the incipient flames. I looked at Carlos to see if he was shooting this whole process, but he was changing tapes in the camera in anticipation of a long interview.

Gigi was rearranging the wood around now that the fire was blazing. I was surprised at how quickly she had made it work. She sat down on the edge of the yellow couch and stared intently into the flames. Her features looked even more striking in the amber light. Her dark eyes surrounded by the thick eyeliner and the dark red lips gave her the appearance of a mask from an Asian puppet theater. Suddenly, I could see her enigmatic beauty as a door through which one could enter and follow strange journeys. I wondered if the 'tricks' who sought transvestites felt like this when they saw her in the streets, or were just driven by blind lust.

Carlos pointed the camera at Gigi and looked at me.

'Why don't you hold the shotgun mic and make sure you direct it to her mouth as much as possible?' he said.

I took the microphone from his hands and held it in Gigi's direction. Carlos tended to take upon himself all the technical details in our shoots while I found myself getting lost in directorial reverie, thinking how to shoot a scene. So every time Carlos asked me to take care of something technical I was reminded of how much he worked behind the scenes and how our skeleton crew operation tended to be unfair towards him.

'Gigi, tell us about the street,' I asked, realizing immediately what a dumb general question I had posed. But Gigi chose her direction quickly.

'Money comes real easy our way 'cause there's many men out there who appear to be one thing in society and then feel secretly passionate for another. You know, married men who have feelings for their own sex, and come looking for us at night. And once they're paid up with us it's a sealed deal and no one finds out, 'cause it's nobody's business out there in society.'

The thing about Gigi's speech was that, although she came from an uneducated background, her choice of words and grammatical structure in Spanish were exquisitely poetic. I would only learn later that Caribbean people tend to weave poetry into their every day speech, in particular Puerto Ricans who account for the highest percentage of poets in the region. But at this moment, I was just deeply touched by some of her expressions like 'secretly passionate' and 'sealed deals'. I was also surprised at the way she talked about society as something 'out there' where she didn't belong, a place she could only contemplate from the fringes.

'How is it working and living in the street?' I asked.

'Life in the street is sad. I have friends who work in the street but then go back home 'cause they don't have a substance problem. But for us it's different. Sleeping in the street is really tough.' Her voice had gotten thinner and her eyes were shining. I felt my eyes stinging too and for a moment, I was afraid I would be pulled into her emotion.

'And many of the men are good,' she continued, 'But one has to be very careful. Every other day one of us is found strangled in an abandoned car or a hotel room.'

Her words suddenly opened a sinister window into the underworld she inhabited. I felt a pang of fear for her.

'Wouldn't it be safer to hustle as a male?' I asked and immediately realized I was overstepping boundaries. Gigi gave me a look.

'Why would I dress as a male if I don't feel like one?' she said dryly.

'How long have you been dressing as a woman?'

I knew I was navigating dangerous waters but I desperately wanted to start a conversation about her sexual identity.

Gigi stared at me, her gaze like a defiant shield.

'It's not just about dressing. I am a woman encased in the body of a man. This is how I've always been. When I came out at thirteen and told my mother, she tried everything. She took me to a psychiatrist, but after a few sessions he said, *Don't even try. She is a woman in the body of a man.* But my mother became frustrated and threw me out. I have been living in the street ever since.'

She paused for a moment and I held my breath. I wanted to empathize with her, give her some soothing words, but I resisted. Something told me that I had to let her process her own thoughts without interference.

After a beat she shook her head, and said, 'I will never forgive my mother. But I have no regrets. Before I left I was working and gave her all my money. Even living on the street I managed to finish high school—so I didn't do that badly, did I?'

She uttered this last question with immense sadness, and then turned to the bonfire where her dark amber eyes flickered with the dancing flames.

As we would soon realize, Gigi was the most passionate and emotional of all the drag queens we were to meet in *The Salt Mines*. She was the only one who professed being in a love relationship with her partner, Edwin. That night she talked about her passion for Edwin and told us she was waiting for him to be released from prison. All these weeks she had been holding onto a leather jacket she had come across which she intended to give him as a present when he got released. To avoid the risk of having it stolen, she had been wearing the leather jacket night and day as the only means of securing it.

'The only way to hold on to it is never to take it off your body,' she laughed rubbing the leather on her chest. Talking about Edwin lifted her mood.

She told us that when they were together they worked as a team. Gigi did tricks and Edwin protected her as much as possible on the street. For instance, when she got into a car with a client, he made a note of the number plate. At the end of the night they always shared Gigi's earnings. I wasn't sure if she was describing Edwin as her pimp, but I didn't know how to ask without annoying her.

'We're in this vice together, you see,' she explained noticing my hesitation.

After a moment I pushed on.

'Is being a woman the way you feel towards Edwin? I mean, how is the way you love Edwin different than the way any regular gay man loves his lover?'

She looked at me fiercely.

'You know, love between two men is much stronger than love between a man and a woman. Love between two men is the deepest love there is. Edwin has cut his veins every time I have tried to leave him. Love between two men is the *most* passionate love that exists.'

She spoke with arrogant rage and held my gaze as if she expected me to bow to her words. It was a female-to-female act of defiance. *My love is better than yours.* I felt a sting. At that time, my love connection with Carlos was very deep. It felt strange to be excluded from the world of passion because of our gender. It took me a moment to realize that Gigi was coming from utter bitterness towards a world that had cast her out because of her sexual choices.

We were all silent for a while. It was a moonless night and a trail of tiny stars glittered far into the dark sky. It felt miles away from the city, from the luminous pollution of the urban streets, its torrent of worldly dealings and crowds of citizens living by the same rules. *The Salt Mines* had a way of being a closed world within the larger world, a sort of mine shaft into the human heart.

Later on when we walked away from *The Salt Mines*, I felt for the first time what would later become the staple sensation every time we ended a shoot and left. The conflicting feeling of trying to articulate an ice-numb body, a pumping heart, and a feverish brain. There was always that struggle between wanting to go there to capture that reality in film ––a reality that we knew could vanish any moment— and then once there, wanting to bolt, to flee away from the miserable situation these fellow human beings were immersed in.

That night, I was sleepless with Gigi's words playing over and over in my mind. I thought about how she had described her love for Edwin, and how it made sense that being homeless, estranged from family and country, and hooked into prostitution as the only means to provide for drugs, Edwin would become the sole intense object of her affection. They had nothing in the conventional sense of the word, nothing material, no social standing. They only had each other. And every day they walked on razor blades between disease, prison, drugs and death. With such high stakes, how immensely passionate could their love be?

Moreover, their love wasn't just an act of disobedience against par-

ents, conventional communities or societal norms. Refusing to accept
your given sexual gender, declaring to be a different gender encased in
a given body was something else. It was one of the most rebellious acts
of defiance in the face of existence.

All of this made me reflect on my own sexual identity. I was thirty-
two years old at the time and I had no doubts about my femininity or
heterosexual preference. But I had many questions about the depth of
female identity. It was already clear in the general culture that being a
woman was not just being a wife or a lover, or even a mother, although
one could be all those things. It was also clear that women could com-
pete with men in the marketplace or in academia and the arts at equal
levels. But it wasn't really clear what else it was to be a woman. Not
just what separated us from men, but what made us unique. What was
the essence of womanhood? Although it sounds strange, I think I was
looking for some of these answers in *The Salt Mines*.

I t was essential to make a fire each time we went to *The Salt Mines*.
Otherwise, it was just too cold and miserable to have anyone talk on
camera for any length of time. So every time we arrived and found
someone to interview we immediately went about building a fire. We
also brought food and drinks always. Coffee and hot chocolate were fa-
vorites, bagels and sandwiches too. If we came in towards the late afternoon or the evening, we sometimes brought whole roast chickens and
cans of beer or coke. This was essential for more than one reason. First,
providing food creates trust and a sense of warmth between people. It
also becomes an incentive to sit down and talk to the camera. But in this

case, it was vital when dealing with cold and hungry homeless subjects.

However, there were some times when we got to *The Salt Mines* and the bonfire was already blazing and a group of drag queens and other companions were sitting around, eating and drinking, like a family hanging out together in the living room.

This was the kind of scene we encountered the next day we went down to shoot. Four of them were sitting on crates, boxes, and the staple dirty golden corner sofa, warming themselves around the fire. Giovanna, and three others we didn't know: Jackie, a wiry drag queen with reddish long hair who was Little Man's 'wife'; Ruben, a young kid who couldn't have been more than sixteen, still dressed as a boy, but with honey-colored dyed hair; and Michael, a slender black youth with mellow eyes and a permanent smile on his lips.

They were all engrossed listening to Giovanna who sat like a queen on the dirty golden sofa with a bag of fancy clothes on her lap. No one seemed to object when we sat down and took out the camera equipment and set about filming. Giovanna was taking the clothes and accessories out of the bag. She took out a party dress and held it up for everyone to see. It was a short blue taffeta strapless dress with a band of glittering beads around the waist. Everyone first gasped and then broke into exclamations.

'Oh, my God!' Jackie said covering her mouth in a dramatic gesture.

'That's a DIE FOR!' exclaimed Ruben.

Giovanna placed the dress against her body and said with a smug look on her face, 'I am going to look sooo beautiful in this!'

'Where did you get the dress?' I asked her.

'*Mi amiguito*—my little friend—Michael got it for me,' she said with a mischievous smile.

I looked at Michael, at his shabby plain clothes, and wondered where he could have gotten an expensive dress like this.

'You know, he went on a *special* shopping spree at Lord & Taylor's,' Giovanna chuckled

Michael stared back at me with smiling amber eyes. There was no guilt or apology in his gaze.

Giovanna folded the dress neatly and took out a custom rhinestone headband and a faux diamond bracelet and tried them on.

'These are the accessories I am going to wear with the dress. Aren't they awesome? All of this reminds me of when I started dressing,' she lowered her head and added with a deep nostalgia, 'It seems so long ago!'

There was a moment of silence in the group which I took for a sign of respect towards Giovanna's heartache. But then I realized that something else had suddenly shifted the whole attention of the group. I noticed they were whispering among themselves and looking off to the right. Then I saw a guy standing a few yards away, facing one of the trucks while he smoked something. When I looked closer I saw he was pulling greedily from his smoke and I noticed the hard look in his black eyes. We stood by the group with the camera, but waited cautiously. Giovanna and the others were totally glued to the scene. Finally, Giovanna whispered something in Ruben's ear and then nudged him to get up and go talk to the smoking stranger. Ruben went up to him and charmingly invited him to join the group. The guy put away his smoking materials, came over and sat on one of the crates looking shyly towards the group.

'Hey, want some coffee?' said Giovanna with a flirty flair, and offered him one of the coffees we had brought.

'What's your name?'

'They call me JR,' he answered shyly. He was a medium build guy in his early thirties and wore what could have been a neat navy shirt a couple of days ago, but now looked as totally dishevelled as the rest of his appearance. His ashen complexion spoke of sleepless nights and his intense black eyes of endless obsession.

I sat in front of Giovanna.

'Tell me about crack.'

'You want to know about crack?' Her smile was taunting, her big brown eyes had a way of scanning mine with a mix of malice and mirth.

'Are you sure? You know, it's the most addictive thing in the world. *Irresistible.* You might end up asking me to go get you some. And then—HA! We would have some kind of a situation.'

'You mean I would become a crack addict just like that?'

'You could.'

'I wouldn't let her,' intervened Carlos who was adjusting the sound levels and getting ready to shoot.

'You wouldn't?' Giovanna repeated opening her eyes wide. 'You don't know anything about crack. That drug is SOMETHING! I have seen married men take off their wedding rings and say, *Bring me more.* I have seen kids take off their sneakers and coats in the middle of winter for that drug. THAT is crack cocaine'

'But what does it do? What does it make you feel? Why is it so addictive?'

Giovanna laughed her raspy laugh and sucked on her teeth as if she were preparing to reveal something astonishing. Then she looked at me with fire in her eyes: 'They say that when you have an orgasm there is something in your brain, a fluid of some kind, that gets released. Right? So when you smoke crack, that same fluid in the brain gets released too. So imagine, every time you take a hit, it's like you're coming… It HAS to be addictive, don't you think?'

'Hey, that's not a bad way of putting it,' intervened JR, looking at her thoughtfully.

'And what is your experience with crack?' I asked him while Carlos swung the camera in his direction. I was taking a risk by asking him a question on camera without having first secured his consent to be filmed. Many people refuse to be on camera spontaneously. But the situation was developing in such a casual way that I decided to ride the wave and see how it unfolded.

'That stuff drives me completely crazy,' he answered looking me in the eye. 'I start smoking and after a while all I want is to do is hit people. It's insane.'

Of course, this was the second—and not the least—risk we were taking. JR had just been smoking crack and he could just turn violent and attack us or break our equipment. I thought about it then, and I'm sure Carlos was thinking about it too, but the fact that this guy was actually admitting to his violent behavior was somehow a guarantee that a certain truce would be respected. Self-reflection and impulsive behavior hardly ever coexist simultaneously. But JR was also using our filming for his own purposes: he needed to relate his story of crack madness, his enslavement to this fiend substance that turned him into a brute. And telling a camera is telling the whole world, without being judged by one individual person. This concept of the healing power of telling your story to a camera is something that would take me years to understand in depth. The respect and fascination that a camera elicits in most people is amazing. There is something impersonal and at the same time intimate and universal in a filming camera. There is something of setting a record, of leaving a print in the hall of histories of human beings. There is also the few minutes of limelight. The golden opportunity for all unsung heroes that most of us are.

'That drug has gotten the best of me. This is my third day without going back home,' he turned his face away and stared into the distance. This was the moment to ask him about home, and about who might be waiting for him after three days. But his hard black eyes were telling me he had already spoken too much. He could be on camera and confess to violent behavior but he couldn't be taken home right now. So we turned the camera away discreetly. The transvestites around the bonfire had been listening to him but now also turned their gaze away. They knew very well what he was talking about. There was a moment of heavy silence in the group.

We sat sipping coffee and sharing the warmth of the fire. The fire bonded us silently into a strange sense of brotherhood. There were those who were castaways in this surreal island of *The Salt Mines*, and there was us who dared to tread into their forbidden territory with a camera. And what united us that very moment was a sense of awe for their dramatic journey.

Ruben broke the spell.

'Hey, look whose coming our way! It's Bobby. Hey, Bobby, we need water! You need to go to the hydrant. Yoooe!' Bobby passed by the group without apparently paying any attention. 'Come on, Bobby!' Ruben cooed. Bobby soon reappeared with his emblematic wrench and two big plastic containers. We stood up and asked him if we could film him getting water. He nodded his head in agreement eyeing us shyly and smiling. With a quick look at each other, Carlos and I decided that we needed to split up. He needed to follow Bobby and I needed to stay by the fire and bond with everyone else, gathering information and ideas for the next shooting scene. Of course, I was dying to follow Bobby with the camera to the hydrant. Besides being already frozen and wanting to move around, I anticipated an amazing scene. But this was the way

Carlos and I worked together. We always knew when to split and work separately, and when we needed to be together. That, and the fact that just by looking into each other's eyes we could agree on how to approach the mood of a scene or how to move into a subject with a camera, made us a great working team on location. The fights and discussions would come later in the editing room, but on location, we were a seamless act.

The scene that Carlos filmed with Bobby that day is, in my opinion, one of the most visually beautiful in the whole final documentary. On a deserted street close to the highway the camera strides swiftly towards Bobby who is opening the street hydrant with the oversized wrench. It is one of those clear New York winter mornings with ice blue skies and glittering sun rays. The crisp light gleams over Bobby's widened smile as he wrings the last notch on the huge bolt and the water suddenly spurts out sparkling in the freezing air and splashes over the cobbled stones. The camera swerves around Bobby's strong bare hands plugging the plastic bottles into the hydrant's gurgling spout. It then tilts up to Bobby's face, his watery eyes torn between the wind and his pride at being filmed. I have watched this scene probably over a thousand times and each time I'm struck by its beauty. Carlos was an awesome cameraman, his camera work was subtle and sensuous at the same time. His movements were fluid and graceful. He knew when to frame a tight shot of a face filled with emotion, and when to zoom out into a larger picture of the situation. His presence behind the camera was friendly and relaxing; he could be the fly on the wall or the understanding stranger to whom you want to tell your entire life story.

Back in *The Salt Mines*, Bobby delivered the water to Ruben and the others.

'You should shoot Bobby's truck,' Ruben said. 'He has the most amazing place in the whole Salt Mine.'

This, of course, didn't necessarily mean much, but actually we ended up being pretty impressed by Bobby's 'place'. He had chosen a truck without extensive body damage whose interior could be accessed through a functioning door. He had cleaned out the inside of the truck and placed an actual bed, covering it with a real bedspread. We stepped up after him and flooded the room with the camera light. From the inside the space felt much larger than I had imagined. It was tidy, with folded clothes stacked neatly together with other personal objects on a few wooden shelves on the side.

'Come on Bobby,' said Ruben from the door, 'Show them the radio,'

Bobby pointed to an old radio by the side of the bed. He tweaked some cables and a romantic song blasted out of the small speakers. Bobby beamed.

'I hooked it up to a car battery,' he said bashfully.

'Isn't it great?' drawled Ruben and with a sprightly jump he hauled himself into the truck and stretched out his limbs lazily across the bed like a cat.

'I am also working on installing a small wood-burning stove I found around,' continued Bobby, 'I'm thinking of opening a hole up here to hook up a vent pipe. But pipes aren't easy to come by around here.' His face was flushed with excitement.

'How come you ended up here?' I asked.

'Well…' he wavered. 'I'm not like these guys. I don't do drugs. I work, I find antiques around and sell them.'

'OH, PLEASE! Not this whole thing again. You are so full of it,' drawled Ruben in mock annoyance, 'I'm leaving. I won't hear this one more time.' He got up and left in obvious jest.

'But we're like a family. We're look out for each other,' Bobby added.

Sitting on the edge of the bed, he told us a few things about his life. In the past he had worked for the Sanitation Department, but had gotten laid off a while ago. He had more recently been released from prison, and had failed to reinsert himself back into his family or get a job that would pay for basic expenses. He had a small daughter whom he missed but he was waiting to get his life together again before he could even think of approaching his ex-wife. He told us all this in a discreet but dignified manner. I wanted to ask him why he had been in prison, but I felt I might embarrass him so I didn't. From what he told us I figured he might have been involved in some petty theft. I also wanted to ask him if he used crack like the others but didn't, because he had openly denied it in the beginning. The difference between Bobby and the drag queens was that they were shamelessly forthcoming with all kinds of personal information, whereas Bobby felt that he had a reputation that had to be kept as intact as possible.

That afternoon, we returned to our apartment in Chelsea, and before we had time to take off our coats or put down the equipment, the doorbell rang. It was our friend Idoia and her boyfriend Max. She was a dancer studying with Martha Graham's company at the time. A beautiful dark slender woman from the Basque Country. We asked them to come up and prepared coffee. Because both Carlos and I were so enthralled with our experience shooting down at the pier, we couldn't help telling them about *The Salt Mines* and the Salt people. They listened in fascination. Then Idoia asked to see some of the images. Against all rules of never showing footage off the master tapes in case they get damaged in the playback, we were just too excited to resist and went ahead and showed them a few seconds of material. We played back the scene were Giovanna was showing her dress to the camera.

'I could have never imagined anything like this to exist,' said Idoia, 'And where is this guy from?' she asked, pointing at Giovanna.

'She's from Dominican Republic—they're all from different Caribbean countries, some grew up in New York,' I said.

'Why do you call them *she?* They're men, aren't they?'

For the first time I realized that I was calling them *she's* instead of *he's.*

'Yes, they are men,' I mumbled, 'but they feel like women, so what can I call them?'

'You mean *they want to be women.* But they're still men, so they should still be called *he.'*

Idoia was very passionate and opinionated in her views. Now she was being very stubborn and refusing to accept the Salt Queens as feminine. Yet, she was bringing up an interesting point. Why was I addressing them as women? Did I actually perceive them as more feminine than masculine? In a way, yes. They didn't feel like average women any more than they felt like average men, but they took on a feminine persona that was hard to ignore. Or was it about bonding with them? In another way, yes. How could I gain their trust if I approached them in a way that dismissed the image they were trying so hard to project to the world? However I argued these points, I failed to change Idoia's beliefs on the subject. To her, addressing men as women was inappropriate, no matter what they felt, or what they requested.

This question would come up many times later when I showed the finished documentary to a variety of audiences. There was always someone among the viewers who would question the *she.* The answer I learned to give was this: if you are going to treat somebody with respect you need to call them whatever they want to be called. The deeper meaning of the name or the address is up to them, not to you. This had been one of my deeper lessons during the shooting in *The Salt Mines*.

One of the riddles that *The Salt Mines* posed for me was how drag femininity compared to and was different from women's. It may sound bizarre, but being in close contact with drag queens all those weeks made me very aware of what separated us and what united us. Another question that kept going over and over in my mind was, why did they want to be women in a world that was still largely dominated by men? To be born a woman is one thing, but to turn into one against all odds and be relegated to the narrowest fringe of female definition was another. But was it the narrowest?

I was coming from the place of a woman who had been born and raised in a culture not just male-dominated, but also Roman Catholic. My perception growing up was that women didn't quite make the mark and therefore had to try harder at everything. And although we did and succeeded, there was always a vague sense of exclusion from the privileged position of men. But here I was, in front of men who felt very different. Their passion was to seek life in the feminine.

Whenever back in the apartment I looked at myself in the mirror, I thought about what separated me physically from the Salt Mine drag queens besides our congenital sexes.

I wore my dark hair short, Louise Brooks style, a dramatic bob with bangs over my long eyebrows and hazel eyes. They, by contrast, always

wore longish hair, mostly colored blonde or red, as an essential feminine feature in their appearance. My face was round, with pale, slightly freckled skin and a small nose and mouth. They, by contrast, had
larger and more dramatic features, bigger eyes and noses, thicker lips.
Everything that came from importing their male features into the cru-
cible of feminine transformation. They also wore exuberant makeup,
thick eye liner and layers of mascara, intense red lipstick. I hardly wore
any makeup at all. Their clothes, when they dressed for the occasion,
were explicitly sexy or even explosive. Their bodies, although slender
like mine, were bonier, but when they dressed up they looked curvier
and definitely more voluptuous. It might have had to do with the way
they moved, swaying hips, walking affectedly by placing one foot in
front of another. Sometimes plainly slithering along, like snakes hyp-
notizing prey. And then, the way they flirted and threw themselves at
the men! How they batted their eyelids, blew noisy kisses or paid erotic
compliments before they burst out laughing in their faces. I was much
more demure, and so were all the women I knew. But they seemed to
have no boundaries, no fear.

'Well, of course,' was Idoia's simple explanation, 'They don't get
pregnant!'

'Well, they don't. But they can also get killed or abused by men,' I
said.

'Sure, like any other prostitute, male or female,' she retorted.

'So you think pregnancy and childbearing are the main difference?'

'Of course.'

'And what are the similarities?'

'There are no *real* similarities. They're just caricatures of women.'

Idoia always acted as the devil's advocate when it came to the Salt
Queens. Talking to her had a sobering effect on my torturing thoughts.

But only because she echoed mainstream perception. I understood everything she said, but I still felt there was a deeper meaning to it all. A door into an unexplored, mysterious pocket of reality that I just had to open and go through.

The more I thought about these topics of gender identity the more interesting I found the story of *The Salt Mines*. One day I remembered a strange scene of one of Federico Fellini's movies called *Satyricon* in which there was an albino hermaphrodite inside an ancient Greek oracle cave. The albino hermaphrodite was the actual source of the oracle, and therefore a conduit for clairvoyant information into the human world. At the time of seeing this movie, I had learned that in many cultures, hermaphrodites and transgendered people were considered divine or even superior to ordinary men and women, just because they integrated both masculine and feminine elements.

I started going to the Central Library to do some research whenever I was free. At that time, modern literature on transgender or even homosexual topics was not as abundant as now. I plunged into the study of worldwide myths and was surprised to find out that many cultures around the world, including Classical Greek, have granted a special space for beings with different sexuality. Many of these cultures have attributed divine or extraordinary qualities to those beings who are neither male nor female but belong to both. Finally, I came across an amazing documentary segment that had been produced by a BBC program called *Everything Under the Sun*. It was a story shot in South India with a community of Hijra nuns, all of whom were transgendered males, some born hermaphrodites—or, as we now call them, intersex—and others who were castrated males or just transsexuals. These Hijras not only dressed and acted as women, but also believed they were women incarnated in the bodies of men. They lived together in some sort of congregation in a small monastery and were supported by the community who believed they had divine powers conferred to them by their special sexuality. These Hijra nuns attended public events and blessed weddings and births, as well as harvests and other community events. The documentary also explored the fact that this caste of transgendered beings either acted in this type of religious role or was confined to the role of prostitution and begging on the streets. Sometimes the stepping stone into the monastery life was castration.

Although the topic was largely approached from an anthropological point of view, it was a mind-blowing film. But the question that immediately opened up in my mind was, if this situation has been going on since the dawn of society, and if other cultures have managed to integrate it, what have we done with it in Western society? The West has suppressed any sexuality that was not deemed to integrate a strict male-female family pattern. The only alternative form of sexuality allowed has been devised by religion as those *eunuchs who make themselves so for the service of God* (Matthew 19:12), meaning the men and women who embrace chastity to become nuns, monks or priests. What happened to those others who didn't conform to this strict classification of gender? They were just condemned to exist hidden away, surviving on the fringes of mainstream culture.

When Carlos saw the documentary, he was also impressed.

'I guess when humans can't explain something rationally, they just bring in the divine.' He was a die-hard pragmatist.

What fascinated me most was the concept that the combination between male and female produced not just a mixture between the two, but a new being endowed with superior, more powerful qualities. Qualities that couldn't be developed in systems where they were considered degenerate beings. But even under those circumstances, the potential qualities were still there.

I t was a cold but clear day. The white winter sun dazzled the surfaces of the old trucks covered in thin layers of ice. There was no one around. We went over to the truck we had finally identified as Gigi's abode but no one responded when we knocked on the metal surface or called her name. Again, I got that queasy feeling in my stomach about trespassing in this cemetery of garbage trucks and facing the possibility of returning empty handed to the outside world. The uneasiness always subsided when we met with any of the inhabitants of *The Salt Mines*. They provided the only safe conduct into this unbearable side of reality.

I walked around a bit. Giovanna had promised the day before she would meet with us and talk to the camera. But I was quickly learning that promises are not always possible to keep when you live in the streets.

Suddenly I heard a clinking sound at the far end behind the last line of trucks. I thought it might be just the wind banging on some metallic surface. It was always like this in *The Salt Mines*. Against a backdrop of eerie silence, the wind whistled through metal crevices or hollow pipes, flapping and banging plastic or Styrofoam pieces, or just pouring its icy breath noisily through every nook and cranny in the compound.

I walked in the direction of the clinking sound. At the far end of the enclosure, close to the gate by the river, there was a large mound of what looked like demolition debris covered with garbage. And on top of it, a lanky figure in a shabby green coat was poking around the rubble. I recognized Giovanna.

'Hey! I thought you had blown me off for the day.'

She looked up and smiled.

'Well, I nearly did. I tried to convince a trick to take me to a hotel for the night—but it didn't work, so I had to come back in the end,' she said with a sigh.

She stared intently into the rubbish at her feet.

'What are you looking for?'

'Oh, I'm looking for a spoon.'

'A spoon?' I said in surprise.

'Yeah, a spoon,' she repeated distractedly, and then, 'Hey, here it is!' and she swooped down and emerged with a spoon in her hand. I saw that she was carrying an empty can in the other hand. It looked like a medium sized paint can.

'Why do you want a spoon?'

'I'm making hot chocolate today. My friend Michael just brought some chocolate powder and milk. I was going to heat up the milk.'

'You're kidding. We brought coffee and bagels.'

'The thing is I *really* want chocolate today. What to do, I'm an addict. An addict of more substances than one,' she added laughing while she tottered down the mound, her feet fumbling tentatively for safe stepping surfaces among the rubbish.

Back in the main clearing among the trucks, Carlos had already started a fire. Today, alongside with coffee and bagels, we had brought a bag of women's clothes. I had rounded up a few girlfriends and asked them to donate nice clothes they didn't wear anymore. Everyone had been generous and I had collected a few bags. As soon as we got to the fire I handed the bags to Giovanna. She opened one and sifted quickly through the items trying this one and that one on, shrieking in delight. I immediately realized we should have set up the camera before I gave her the clothes because it was an amazing scene to shoot. But it was too late. I saw how hard it was to relate spontaneously towards the person you want to film while planning for the best way to shoot at the same time. It would take me years to learn to balance these two planes of operation in a shoot, and even then, there was always having to choose between being the friend or the producer. It is hard to be the observer and participate in the action at the same time.

In the meantime, Giovanna had picked out a faux fur hat, with matching scarf and gloves from the bag. She uttered a thousand thank yous while she folded the rest of the items neatly and put them back into the bag. Then she disappeared for a moment, to store the clothes safely in her truck, she said.

A few minutes later she was sitting back again by the fire clad in her newly acquired goodies. She crossed her legs in studied feminine fashion while she waited for the camera to be ready.

I wanted to ask questions related to her sexuality following up on some of the topics that had come up in Gigi's last interview.

'How does it feel to be a woman?' I asked her.

'OOOh it feels real good! I just loooove dressing and putting on makeup, buying clothes and accessories. Well, these days, more than buying one would say *shoplifting*,' she added lowering her voice while her eyes flashed mischievous glances around as if there might be someone listening in on our conversation.

'And besides clothes, what is it that makes you feel like a woman?'

'Besides clothes! Well, that's one of the best parts, isn't it?'

'No really, what else makes you feel like a woman?'

She looked at me for a moment and then laughed coyly, 'I guess it's about wanting to be a woman for the man I love.'

'Like what?'

'Like dressing up and looking beautiful, like waiting for him when he comes home after work, cooking amazing meals– I don't know, all those things…'

'What else is being a woman?'

'Hey! This is a real hard question. You're squeezing my brain today.'

I was. I knew it was a near to impossible question. But my fascination with transvestites had to do with finding out what they thought being a woman was. Somewhere inside I felt they might have the key to some crucial information about female identity.

Giovanna sighed.

'Okay, let me tell you something. There's men who love men and they are just gay men. Then there's men who feel like women and of course love men, and who want to become women for them. But then there's me. I'm a transvestite to the full. I love my breasts—my silicone breasts,' she smirked, 'But I adore my penis, too—so that's it! I'm the best of both worlds, a transvestite to the full.'

Giovanna paused for a moment. Her smile was frozen on her face and her eyes continued to search mine. I saw a spark of doubt flashing in their depth. It came with a sort of anguish. But I knew the doubt didn't come from what she had just said. She had no doubts about her identity. What she doubted was whether I could understand and accept her the way she was—to the full.

She started poking the burning wood with a stick, lost in thought. After a moment she started speaking again in a more subdued tone of voice.

'When I first started dressing up, I lived with a guy who took care of me completely. I dropped out of school. I left everything for him. And my sister used to say, be careful, 'cause if he leaves you, you'll have nothing to fall back on. And that's what happened. He left and I ended up in the streets.'

She poked the fire again for a while. Then, suddenly looked up again and laughed.

'But you see, I've always been like this. When I was a kid I played with dolls and wore my mother's shoes up and down the stairs. And when we played house, I had to be the mother—otherwise, there was no game.'

Giovanna tended to cover her mouth when she laughed. She also sucked on her teeth when she was in total splits. She was probably conscious of the wide gap between her front teeth and the fact that one of them was chipped. But most of her mirth was expressed through the eyes. She had deep black eyes that could dance with laughter as intensely as they could pierce with hatred or empty out with gloom. She was witty and extremely intelligent. These two qualities were the ground of her charisma. She commanded respect and admiration and had her retinue of followers in *The Salt Mines*, particularly Michael and Ruben who seemed to be at her beck and call. By contrast, Sara, even as feminine as she was, was more the patriarchal presence in the community, someone to seek out when there were serious problems. Gigi, on the other hand was an independent member of the group, although her allegiance steered more towards Sara.

We heard soft footsteps approach and looked up.

'Michael!' exclaimed Giovanna.

Michael turned shyly towards us with a broad smile. We had met him a few days ago. He was a lean teenager with short Rasta locks shooting out around his head. His amber eyes contrasted with his ebony skin.

'Hey Gio, where's the famous chocolate milk?' His voice was mellow and teasing.

'Oh shit! I forgot everything about it!'

Giovanna jumped up from her crate and looked around for the paint can and the spoon she had collected on the rubbish mound.

Once she found them, she rinsed them out with water from a bottle nearby, while Michael fixed the fire to accommodate the pot. Giovanna poured milk from a carton and mixed in the chocolate powder with the spoon. Michael helped her place the can over the flames.

'I know what you're thinking,' said Giovanna looking at me with a smirk. 'But the moment the milk boils it will be okay. You know what they say, *lo que no mata, engorda*, if something doesn't kill you, it fattens you,' she said in Spanish and winked an eye at me.

'It'll be all right.' said Michael, laughing softly.

It took more than thirty minutes to heat up the concoction. When it was ready, Giovanna offered us some in paper cups, but we gracefully declined and sipped our cold coffees. Bringing food on the shoots was one thing, but eating with them was another. It was very hard for Carlos and I to eat anything inside *The Salt Mines*. The surrounding garbage, the desolate landscape, the tension of the filming made knots in our stomachs. Drinking coffee was all we could manage.

'Aren't you eating with us?' they would ask every time.

We always made some excuse, we already ate, we're meeting friends for dinner. But I was mortified at the idea that our repugnance would hurt their feelings. However, they probably understood. There was never any reproach, only warmth and gratitude every time we came around with any gift.

L ater in the afternoon, after Giovanna and Michael had finished the whole can of hot chocolate, they brought out the bag of clothes and looked at them one by one. Most of them were colorful woolen sweaters and scarfs. There were also fancy pantyhose with designs, and leg warmers.

I turned to Carlos, 'Let's shoot this!'

'We're out of tapes,' he said looking at me wearily.

'You're kidding! That's impossible,' I said and dived into the production bag in a frantic search to prove him wrong. But he was right, there were no tapes to be found.

'How could this *be*?' I asked in frustration.

'Remember I asked you to take care of the tapes back in the apartment?' he said patiently.

It suddenly hit me. I had left a second stack of tapes on the kitchen table and totally forgotten about them. I had been totally engrossed packing up the clothes for the Salt Queens. I sat dejected watching Giovanna and Michael trying on colorful scarves and sweaters in a festival of girly shrieks and laughter. The scene we would never have on tape was so beautiful, I wanted to cry.

Carlos squeezed my arm.

'*Así es la vida*, such is life,' he said soothingly, 'Anyway, I'm knackered, I don't think I could have filmed any more today.' He had been working until late the night before, but I knew he was only saying this to console me. Carlos was quite tireless when it came to shooting.

We watched as Giovanna and Michael finally settled on the attire they were going to wear for the evening. Both looked totally revamped as they wore the new sweaters over their old dirty ones and covered their dishevelled heads with wool hats. They finally took off together towards the street chattering cheerfully. They were going on a 'mission' they said.

At that time I still didn't know anything about the street drug language. Later on I would find out that "going on a mission" meant going off on a quest for drugs, crack in particular, and that the mission could end up being a complicated journey, sometimes taking up to a few days.

As we were preparing to leave ourselves, Gigi suddenly walked in and sat by the fire, looking crestfallen.

'Everything all right?' I asked her.

'Not if you consider I spent the whole day at the Rock and never made it past the visitor's line!'

'The Rock?' I ventured.

She lifted her eyes and looked at me in wonder. 'You don't know the Rock? Rikers Island? The largest prison around? That's where Edwin is. Or was. I hope they haven't transferred him to the Federal'

All this prison talk was new to me. I was about to say, *Would you tell us about all this on camera?* when I remembered about the tapes again. Another great scene lost. I brooded bitterly about the fact that I would probably never get a second chance at filming scenes like these. I was painfully aware of how ephemeral everything was in this world of *The Salt Mines*, how soon it would all dissolve away. Production mistakes were just fatal.

We gave her the leftover bagels and coffee and left.

The next time we came down to *The Salt Mines* ready to film, we were surprised to find a large number of the Salt Queens gathered together, all dressed up as if to go somewhere and milling around in spite of the cold wind. No one had lit a fire, no one was sharing food. We went up to Giovanna to figure out what was going on. As we greeted her, I noticed that her eyes flickered nervously between my face and something way behind my back.

Then I heard the chirping voice.

'Hi, How've you been?' A woman we would later know as Yvonne called out.

I turned around and saw them, a single frontal line of eight or nine individuals advancing in unison, like soldiers combing a battlefield. There must have been eight or nine of them, men and women, all ages and races. Most of them dressed in long coats or gabardines, under which the women wore heavy dresses and boots, and the men suits with ties, or turtle necks and plaid pants. Hardly the type of attire desirable or even practical for a place like this. One of them stood out as the leader, a heavy set figure wearing a green parka, advancing in front of the row.

Yvonne wrapped her arms around Giovanna.

'How are you? I missed you!' she chimed.

Her skin was light brown and she had large brown eyes and a prominent nose.

I observed Giovanna's grimace as she submitted to her tight embrace. Then, Yvonne turned around to me.

'Hi, Susana, so nice to meet you!'

I was totally taken by surprise. My brain dashed into a vertiginous scan of events and confused threads of information. Who was this woman and how could she know my name or anything about me? Then it hit me. The two large four wheelers that had broken into the scene a week ago when we brought Thanksgiving leftovers.

Before I could process all this information, another smiling face stepped in front of me with an extended hand.

'So nice to meet you at last. My name is Terry.'

We shook hands. He had big warm hands. His face was wide with large green eyes and he had a silky, silver mustache that matched his thin hair parted on the side. There was an earthiness to him, but there was also a ring of obscure magnetic energy around him. He stared at me smilingly in the eye without flinching. I felt uneasy but held my ground.

'We've been shooting a documentary on homelessness with these guys for the last few days…' I started explaining as if to justify myself.

'I know all about it,' he said, and then added after a beat, 'We're working with them too. We visit them all the time and make sure they're all right. We bring them food and clothes.'

'Oh, so you are working with them? What kind of work?'

He hesitated for a moment.

'We work to help them overcome their troubles.'

The word *troubles* rang in my head with a distinct reformatory note.

'And how do you do that?' I asked.

'Well, we make sure they know we are friends—and brothers and sisters in Christ.'

Of course! Why hadn't I detected it from the beginning! A church coming into *The Salt Mines* for missionary work. My producer brain started processing feverishly—such an amazing addition to the documentary. Up to this point, I hadn't thought of outsiders and their wheelings and dealings inside *The Salt Mines*. Now I suddenly wondered if other 'mainstream' characters might also be wandering into the compound. Police? Social workers? Adventurous customers? But to have a church on a mission with down and out drag queens—where would one find such a meeting between the two far ends of the spectrum?

'Umm, Terry, is it? And what are you planning to do with them today?'

He went back into his beaming smile.

'Oh, we're just going to take them out of the cold and make sure they eat something nice and warm up for a while.'

'Could we follow you and film this?'

His eyes darkened, in spite of his stubborn smile.

'Mmmm. Let's see,' he pretended to think for a moment while he shot a few glances around him. 'I think we would need to talk about it first. Here, let me leave a card with you.'

He fumbled in his pocket and brought out a card.

I gave it a quick glance: *Terry, Pastor, Covenant Church, Dallas.* But I didn't look at it in depth. I couldn't afford to lose momentum with Terry.

'Well, could we at least film you rounding them up and talking to them as you take them away?'

'No, I don't think it will do for today—why don't you call me and we'll set up a time to talk?'

I realized it was a lost cause for the time being. I turned to Giovanna and said in Spanish, *'Te vas a ir con ellos? Me prometiste que íbamos a filmar hoy,'* I reminded her that she had promised to shoot with us today.

She looked at me with some embarrassment and when she was about to open her mouth, Yvonne stepped in. 'Ay, *no te preocupes,* don't worry, you can film any other day. But today we have a dinner party waiting—how could you miss that?' she said staring intently into Giovanna's face. I saw Giovanna's gaze drop.

So, they were all going. And we wouldn't be able to film a thing today.

The wind was picking up and we had been standing without moving at all for too long. It was suddenly freezing. The Salt People were beginning to leave the compound with the members of the church. Gigi was the only one who turned her head and gave us a disgusted look indicating that she really didn't want to go. Slowly, the place emptied out.

I looked at Carlos. I was too cold and disappointed to talk. He shot a quick look at the camera in his hand and winked at me. It was a way of telling me he had filmed something. *Something!* I couldn't wait to get home to play it back.

Back in our apartment, we looked at the footage. Carlos had only been able to film a wide shot of the church people as they advanced through the garbage towards the drag queens. He had also been able to shoot Yvonne embracing Giovanna, and her exaggerated singsong greeting, *Hi, how've you been? I missed you!* It was just a few seconds of tape. Enough to establish their presence in *The Salt Mines*, but nothing to work with in the editing room.

I was already scheming up ways to include these church people in the production.

'I'll call this guy tomorrow. We need to film them at any cost. They really bring another angle to the story,' I said collapsing exhausted on the couch as I always did when we returned from *The Salt Mines*. Our homecoming ritual included kicking off boots, throwing off coats, setting down the equipment, and then hurrying towards the living room while peeling our many layers of winter clothes, in a race to beat one another about who would reach the sofa first and crash head on. Whoever lost made tea or coffee. It was Carlos's turn to make coffee today.

'I'm not sure I want to have anything to do with those guys,' his voice trailed from the kitchen. 'They must be radical Christians or something like that. They're probably Born Again Christians or worse. Visiting transvestites in a garbage dump! What kind of intentions can they have?'

I knew Carlos was passionately anticlerical and had great distaste for the doings of any organized religion. He had disliked them instantly. But this time, I was the cool-headed one for a change. Evangelical missionaries in *The Salt Mines* brought an even more extravagant edge to the story. How had they found out about the drag queens? What was their real agenda with them?

'Whatever intentions they might have makes for a great story. I mean these guys have been dumped by society. And the only people who visit them are a religious radical group. It's fascinating, don't you think?'

Carlos walked into the living room with two steaming mugs of coffee.

'I don't think these people are fascinating by any standard! These people are just the religious right. They're worse than fascists! I can't believe you would give them any type of exposure!'

I looked at him in surprise. Carlos didn't get worked up easily over topics. He really had a problem with these guys. Where was that coming from? We sat for a moment sipping our coffees.

'Look, I don't like the religious right myself. But do you really think we would ever give them any positive exposure? Don't you think they would just be another piece of the crazy, grotesque world of *The Salt Mines?*' I said.

'Well, if you show them doing acts of kindness, bringing coats and food, to a population that's totally down and out, stuck in the garbage…'

'But they do that, they bring them stuff. And I'm sure they do other things that are not quite as sweet and loving as that. Don't you think we need to show what's really going on? The good and the bad? The truth?'

'You know, you are very naïve,' he concluded.

'Me? *Naïve?*' The conversation was heating up.

'Yes, naïve. Don't you know how easy it is to manipulate media? Even the most well intended footage? Do you know that last year I filmed an interview with a Ku Klux Klan group where they expressed horrific views on blacks and the need to exterminate them, and at the end of the shoot they managed to get the producer to give them a copy of the footage, and months later they were airing it all over the South as a piece of propaganda? Yes, they actually ended up using it for their own ends.'

'Why do you think we would end up giving these church guys footage?' I asked him.

'Why do you think they would let us shoot for free?' he retorted.

We sat in silence for a beat. It was the first argument we were having over *The Salt Mines*. I was aware that Carlos had more experience in this field. He was beginning to shoot as a cameraman for European television correspondents and media bureaus. He had been exposed to many interesting situations. I admired him immensely that way. But I wasn't going to let go of the gut feeling that the church story would end up being one of the central pieces of the documentary.

After a moment I said, 'Are you saying we should exclude them totally from the shoot?'

'Look, let's not talk about this anymore. We'll just—whatever!' he said ending the conversation abruptly, 'I need to go to work now.'

After he was gone, I brooded for hours about our conversation. First, I was upset we had disagreed. We never fought. We were so totally fused as a couple—our ideals, our dreams, our desire to transform the world were so in sync, that any divergence felt hurtful. But at the same time some very interesting and challenging ideas had arisen from this critical exchange. For example, the manipulation of images and footage and the responsibility the filmmaker has in any potentially damaging situations. And the idea about portraying the truth. For, what is the truth and who tells it? And to what end? Doesn't everyone have a different truth?

Despite all these ruminations, the next day I decided to call Terry and set up a meeting with him. The phone number on the card was a Texas number. A distant female voice with a Southern accent picked up the phone and took a message saying he would call me back. But he never called me back. I kept calling on and off for the next days. The same voice always answered and took the message but I was never able to reach Terry. Every time I dialed the number the image of the sudden darkening over his smiling eyes returned to my mind, and I realized he had already made up his mind then to bar all contact with us. It felt very frustrating. It was as if he held the power to obstruct the documentary I wanted to make. For the first time I felt I wasn't in control of the reality I needed to film. It made me feel insecure about my capacity to finish the piece. Years later, after encountering many other similar situations, I finally understood that this uncertainty is one of the major demons the producer needs to deal with in order to make a film happen. This is why the producer can never take no for an answer.

I didn't give up calling Terry, but he never called me back.

**N**ext time we went down to *The Salt Mines* we met Giovanna and Gigi sitting by the bonfire. The flames burned high over the splintered pieces of what looked like a battered piece of furniture, an old chest of drawers that crackled noisily as the fire collapsed it.

Both Giovanna and Gigi seemed mesmerized by the blazing spectacle. We sat around the fire with them and made small talk until we felt they could warm up to the camera. We had brought some sandwiches and coffee with us, which they accepted as always. But I noticed Giovanna didn't eat hers right away; she just put it to the side, saving it for later.

I decided to take the opportunity to strike a conversation about the church.

'Not hungry?' I teased, 'Is it that you're being invited to dinner parties every day by your friends?'

Both she and Gigi stared at me in confusion.

'Dinner parties?'

'Well, the last time we were here you went off with them, didn't you?' I continued in a mocking tone.

Giovanna was still looking at me puzzled.

'She means the people from the church,' Gigi explained matter-of-factly as she kicked a piece of wood that was sticking out from the blazing pile.

'Oh, God! The people from the church!' chimed Giovanna, suddenly bursting into laughter.

'There was no dinner party to speak of. Just a few potato chips with soda after a VERY long service we had to sit through on an empty stomach,' added Gigi ill-humoredly.

'Yes, that's mostly what they do. They have us attend their services and then give us a snack while they lecture us on how to convert to religion,' said Giovanna.

'You're kidding!' I started.

I wanted to spur them further into talking about the church.

'Wow, wow, wow—' intervened Carlos, 'Nobody is saying one more word until I set up the camera and the microphone. All this needs to go down.'

And he shot me a reproachful look, although mostly in jest. Of course, I had initiated a very juicy conversation without thinking about filming and it just wouldn't do. I found myself many times in this situation where I got carried away with an amazing scene or conversation and only realized too late that we hadn't captured it on tape. Re-staging scenes never quite works the same as when things happen spontaneously. Carlos was more watchful that I in these situations. So we stalled for a moment while we waited for the camera to be ready.

Although Carlos and I hadn't talked again about the church, there was an unspoken feeling between us that we should lay to rest our differences for the now and keep an open mind. While he was setting up the camera, I racked my brain for ways in which I would approach the topic of the church without creating bias or prejudice. But Giovanna and Gigi launched instantly into a rant.

'They insist on calling me Guillermo. They make me real mad when they call me by my masculine name. I say to them, my name is Gigi. It's Gigi and nothing else. But they don't take any notice, some call me Gigi, others call me Guillermo. Some treat me like a woman, some treat me like a man. I don't get what they're about.' said Gigi.

She was stomping around the fire with a furious look in her face.

Giovanna gave a snort of laughter.

'Oh, God, the church. They're something else. They're good people, you know, they worry about us. They want us to quit drugs—that's not so bad, really—but they also want us to stop being ourselves, to stop dressing as women. They insist that we need to accept that we're men. I said to Yvonne, *I have breasts, how do you want me to start dressing instantly like a man and go around like a man?* And you know what she said? *Don't worry, I'm a nurse, I can take out your breasts.* And it's true, they can be taken out. But who told her I want them out?' She squeezed her small breasts together with both hands under her coat as she spoke.

'What do you think they're after?' I asked.

'Who knows! But just because they give you a plate of food and some clothes, they don't have the right to change you or to tell you what to do!' raged Gigi.

She sat back on her crate with a huff, her face scrunched up with fury. Then she added in a softer tone, 'They should respect us as we are. If it's a heartfelt decision, you may change, but if not..? Are we just going to do what *they* want?'

Gigi always started talking in passionate angry tones and ended up with sad, heartbroken statements. Frequently, her face was a tight mask of defensive might; it sometimes reminded me of one of those sepia photos of proud Native American warriors. But in the depth of her eyes there was always a tenderness, a yearning for a softer world.

Giovanna, on the other hand, had witty disdainful way of exposing facts.

'I think these Christians are looking for recognition in their own church. Just imagine, the Good Samaritans who go out into the world and stumble upon us, a little group of nomads in this Salt Mine, sleeping in trucks, in the worse possible conditions, and they turn us into straight men and women and save us unto the Lord. SHIT! What more could anyone accomplish? That's worth a Noble Prize for each one of them, don't you think?'

She laughed her raspy laugh, sucking through her teeth. A gust of wind swept through the bonfire and threw a cloud of smoke in her face. She choked but continued laughing. Now she was wiping the tears from her eyes with the edge of the pink furry scarf I had brought her the other day, and adjusting her hat over her ears. I was also dying to laugh out loud, but I didn't want my voice recorded, so I just smiled widely to let her know I found it funny. I could only imagine Carlos's glee behind the camera.

Gigi was also laughing. When she laughed loud her laugh had sort of a barking quality that made it very unique. She got up and stoked the fire so it would stop smoking.

After a moment, Giovanna grew silent staring at the fire. Then she said in a different tone of voice, 'Let me tell you something. I'm not even sure there is a God anyway. And if I'm wrong, let them punish me. But with so much poverty, so many people dying of hunger, so much evil in this world, how could God let it all happen? So, maybe it's just a way of manipulating the population, of making us afraid to keep us down. Since people are not afraid of the law, maybe they'll be afraid of God...'

She looked at me wondering if she had gone too far. But there was a hint of malice shining in the depth of her gaze. As if she knew the power of her own wit.

Carlos stopped the camera and beamed. 'Wow, Giovanna!'

It was right up his alley. I have to admit I was impressed myself. I had known from the first time I met her that Giovanna was the most intelligent and educated of them all. But these statements revealed a deeper level of thought.

We sat around while they told stories about the church. The church people came to visit them on Thursdays and Sundays. Mostly, they took them to their church where the congregation was gathered to attend the service. They had them sit in the front pews and everyone—or at least, many of them—were friendly to them or even affectionate, but always patronizing. They felt like mascots in that environment, totally out of place. But they did get food and clothes. And of course, constant 'advice' and encouragement of how to change their ways. These church people were determined to save them.

'Giovanna, tell them what happened with Veronica,' said Gigi.

It was already dark, but Gigi had dragged another couple of large wood pieces into the fire and it was blazing again. I just remembered I had put a six pack of Heineken beer in my backpack earlier on and I took it out now and offered Gigi and Giovanna. We rarely brought beer into *The Salt Mines*. Carlos never drank alcohol while he was at work. Neither did I, really. Although, on this occasion, I was dying to drink with them but I was afraid I would need to pee after a while and was terrified at the idea of going out into the dark by myself among the garbage. So I didn't join them.

'Tell them about Veronica,' repeated Gigi.

Giovanna stared intently into the flames while sipping beer from her can.

'Veronica... Well, what is there to say? They got her!' she said at last.

'Who is Veronica?' I asked, 'What happened to her?'

'Veronica was one of the most beautiful drag queens of downtown. Remember, Gigi? She swept through the streets at night, always in beautiful dresses, getting the best tricks, making all the money. She was the best! She was awesome, with huge blue eyes, long blond hair, white skin and a long, slim body. She had the worst tongue ever! EVIL! The way she used to talk to the Church people. To Terry! Remember that day she told him he was a closet faggot and needed a good fuck in the ass? Hell, was she fresh and wicked!'

Both Gigi and Giovanna sniggered for a moment.

'Well, what happened to Veronica? Where is she now?'

'Veronica died of AIDS. A few months ago. But before that—Well, she got deep into crack and ended up in *The Salt Mines*. That's how we got to know her. She was my roommate in my truck for a while,' Giovanna stopped for a moment.

'And?' I was trying to lead her on so she would tell the story uninterruptedly to the camera, but I was beginning to see that this was a heavy emotional piece for Giovanna.

Gigi stepped in.

'Well, she came down with symptoms and they diagnosed AIDS. Her family disowned her. And then she crumbled. She started getting sick. Remember Giovanna, how she started getting all the ulcers on her skin? Such a beautiful queen!'

'What did the church have to do with it?' I asked afraid they would lose the thread.

'The church took her in and changed her. They promised to help her, to get her an apartment and medical care. But they made her dress as a man, they cut her long blonde hair. And she did it, after laughing at them and spitting in their faces. But the worst part was that they made her come when they visited us at *The Salt Mines*. Well, not HER, it was now HIM. Michael, instead of Veronica. He came and lectured us on our sins and told us how we had to change and become Christians. He was shameless in our faces, after all the things we had done together.' Giovanna was mounting into a rage, her deep resentment suddenly erupting onto the surface.

'You would not believe how easily he blurted out all those lies, as if he had really converted to religion, instead of being forced into it out of desperation. The whole thing was disgusting! And then of course he died anyway, and really fast!' She rearranged her hat as she ended her statement, as she often did after saying things that reaffirmed her opinions. She reminded me of some matronly women who readjust their dress or hairstyle after self-righteous diatribes, and at the time I was amazed at how engrained her feminine mannerisms were.

Giovanna was still quivering with indignation as she finished Veronica's story. There was fear and revulsion in her voice. But more than anything, what came across was bitterness. She was bitter towards Veronica.

'What did you feel when she was talking like that?'

'I felt betrayed—it still fills me with rage.'

Giovanna threw her can of beer into the fire and sat there limp, looking spent. I felt that was it for today. There was not much more we could shoot.

The story of Veronica gave us a deeper perspective of their relationship to the church. It was plain how much they resented the church, how conscious they were of their manipulation. But at the same time, we had seen them run off to the church at the least prompting.

In fact a few days later, after shooting in one of the coldest days we got to experience in *The Salt Mines*, we caught Giovanna stealing away toward the ramp in the pier. She was huddled in her thin green coat, holding its collar against her throat with one hand and her hat with the other, as a way of resisting the freezing wind. She seemed breathless from the cold and her body shivered into spastic little jerks as she pushed forward towards the gate.

Carlos followed her with the camera.

'Where are you going, Giovanna?' he asked as he walked alongside with her, looking through the viewfinder of the camera on his shoulder.

'OH GOD! I'm off to the church,' she replied, water streaming from her eyes and nose.

'Don't tell me you're going to the church! Why are you going?' taunted Carlos.

'Firstly, to get out of this unbearable cold—OH, GOD, FORGIVE ME! And then they're buying me a coat. Who knows, maybe something good will rub off on me!' she laughed bitterly and walked faster.

We could see the massive four wheeler waiting for her at the far end of the pier, its engine purring while the exhaust tube exhaled little puffs of warm smoke.

We stopped in our tracks but kept shooting. We wanted a wide angle shot of Giovanna trotting towards the car against the dramatic backdrop of a crimson sky, blotted out by dark jagged clouds.

A few weeks had gone by since we had started shooting in *The Salt Mines*, although our shooting sprees had been scanty and sometimes the results totally fruitless. And as December arrived, even more stark and gray than the moody gusts of November, and the cold sunk in like ice teeth into the bone, I started to really fear that *The Salt Mines* might now end up deserted any day. It made sense that its inhabitants would soon seek more habitable spaces, even though terrible in other ways, such as homeless shelters or even prison.

Gigi had told me these were the places that people living in the street turned to in their darkest hour of desperation. Homeless shelters were degrading and dangerous. You were treated like human garbage and offered no real protection at night inside its walls. Prison was the hardest bullet to bite, potentially exposing you to real brutality. But sometimes they were the only recourse. Particularly, prison stays were the most convenient for effective drug detoxes. There was a whole how-to-manual passed down orally in the streets detailing lists of misdemeanors that would lead to short prison stays, ideal for such recovery projects. Edwin, apparently was on one of these voluntary leaves of absence. At one point he had gotten so far into crack, developed chronic bronchitis and lost so much weight, that he no longer had the capacity to survive in the street. He then mimicked a car break in front of two cops, got arrested and sentenced to three months at 'the Rock'. After that, he would come out clean, clear minded, even chubby from all the prison grub, and ready to start all over again.

Sara could also be on one of these leaves of absence at this time.

I had been hoping to find Sara every time at *The Salt Mines* since the day after Thanksgiving. But she never seemed to be around. When I asked about her, I would get vague answers about her absence or whereabouts. These were not comfortable questions for the Salt People. I learnt that one of the unspoken rules among them was that no one talks, discloses or wags about another, particularly to *outsiders*. As much as we were welcome in *The Salt Mines*, we were still outsiders. So, no information was shared with us about Sara. I was beginning to think she would elude us for the rest of the shooting.

One Sunday towards the middle of December, we went down to *The Salt Mines* in the afternoon. It was cold but sunny and the wind had abated for the last couple of days. As we approached the enclosure from the gate we saw smoke and heard voices, and knew we probably had a shooting session ahead. There was a large group gathered around the fire and the smell of sizzling meat wafted in all directions.

In the middle of the group I recognized Sara's slim blonde figure. She was standing by the fire, addressing the whole group with a commanding masculine voice.

'I don't think that's fair at all', she was saying, 'The person who brings the trick has to have first choice—IN EVERYTHING!' she ended very emphatically. She struck me like the leader of the group, but how did leadership work like in a place like this? I wondered.

When she turned around and saw us, her voice changed into a singsong feminine tone.

'Look who's here! Our filmmakers! Our tickets to Hollywood!'

She was wearing the tattered camel coat we had seen her in the last time, although it was much shabbier now. Underneath, she wore a pair of thin jeans and a cotton sweater. Her hair was pulled back in a ponytail and a line of her original black hair root was visible alongside her blonde colored hair. Her face was thinner, she had marked dark circles around her eyes and her nose looked pinched.

She walked theatrically towards us, wielding a sort of large cooking fork in one hand.

'HELLO! You are just in time for a hamburger party at the renowned Salt Mines!' She took my hand and kissed it in a gentlemanly fashion. 'SUSANA! I've been waiting to see you for days!'

'You have? Well I thought I had been the one seeking you out for days'

She looked at me for a moment with comic alarm on her face and then broke into laughter. She walked back towards the bonfire, swaggering her hips and singing in Spanish.

'*Fumando espero al hombre que yo quiero*—I smoke while waiting for the man I love,' she drawled.

Back at the bonfire the hamburgers were starting to burn.

'Sara!' Gigi screamed, 'Pass the fork, quick!'

But Sara just turned towards us and started dancing a jig in cabaret style, holding the fork as if it were a long cigarette holder.

'Y *mientras fumo, mi vida yo consumo…* and while I smoke, I consume my life,' she sang, pretending to take puffs at the imaginary cigarette holder. Then she broke up into peals of laughter.

'Don't you agree, Susana?'

Gigi came up behind her and yanked the fork out of her hand. Then she stomped back to the hamburgers. Sara let it go without resistance, a theatrical smile frozen on her face. I had to laugh.

Back at the bonfire, Gigi was frantically flipping the smoking hamburgers.

'So, where do you get the meat for the burgers?' asked Carlos.

'We get it from that big store on 14th Street near the river,' said Gigi busily tending to the frying pan. 'What's the name, Edwin?'

'Western Beef,' a thin voice came from across the bonfire.

'Edwin!' I gasped.

Both Carlos and I looked up and saw a short man dressed in dark clothes sitting across the fire from us. We hadn't seen him before when we beheld the group from afar or even when we walked towards it and sat among them. It was as if he had been invisible and had now suddenly materialized at Gigi's calling. He was staring back at us with a shy grin. He had black wavy hair, dark eyes, pointed nose and cheeks, and a small black goatee. It was an old fashioned male face, with sharp bones and deep eye sockets, the type you find in turn-of-the-century photographs. As I looked closer I saw that he was wearing Gigi's leather jacket. This was proof enough of his identity. In the days to follow, I kept observing Edwin's peculiar ability to become invisible. He was a guy who could stand against a wall, a truck, or the sharp angle of a corner and look like he had blended into the background, but then would suddenly spring back to life with a subtle bodily gesture or the utterance of a single word. I kept wondering if this was a talent he had been born with, or something he might have developed as part of becoming a skilled thief.

Meanwhile, the hamburger production was at its peak. Gigi was now sitting by the frying pot, with a big mass of pink ground meat on a sheet of brown grocery paper on her lap. She was amassing it into hamburger patties with both hands, and then slipping them neatly into the frying pot. Across the bonfire was a large black can exhaling small gusts of steam that got quickly dissolved into the chilled air. I wondered what this pot was for.

The first cooked hamburgers were already being passed around and gobbled up quickly. Other people sat around the fire waiting eagerly for their portion. Besides Gigi, Sara and Edwin, I only knew Jackie, who was huddled in a dirty brown coat with an orange hat pulled down to her ears. Nobody was dressed up or wearing make-up today. Everybody looked spent, hungry and cold.

Carlos had set up the camera discreetly on his lap and was beginning to take shots. Some of the people we did not know averted their faces and looked uneasy. Some moved their crates out of the camera range so as not to be in the shot. I was about to make an announcement that we would not film anyone one who didn't want us to, but after a few minutes the group had relaxed and seemed more comfortable with the situation. I wanted to go back to the topic of how they got the meat.

'We get it when they throw it out because it's passed its date of expiration,' explained Gigi engrossed in patting the meat. 'But it's still good. Sometimes they give it to us, other times we take it out of their garbage containers. Edwin got it this time. It's a big package,' she said, looking up and smiling at Edwin.

Edwin smiled back. He was turning the hamburgers with the long fork and passing them around in paper plates. It looked like Edwin had not just foraged the meat but also some plates and even napkins. He seemed to be not only a thief, but also an able provider for the community. Everybody was eating now. There were a few minutes of silence while everyone wolfed down their hamburgers. I could see the color coming back into their faces, their basic energy start to glow once more around their huddled bodies. They must have been very hungry indeed. Once they finished eating, they threw around their paper plates and wrappings, and some of them wandered off leaving just a few people warming themselves by the fire and talking. It never ceased to surprise me how they dumped their garbage right around where they were sitting or sleeping. Any concept of 'housekeeping' was missing, there were no efforts of keeping trash at bay. Not that I was a great housekeeper in my own apartment, which was mostly a mess, but even in The Salt Mines, my instinct was to establish clean areas away from the general garbage, and work towards creating livable spaces. I learned that this was one of the deep differences between me and them: I was a settler and they were nomads, and to cross the razor's edge between these two categories was what determined homelessness.

I turned to Sara. 'Are we going to shoot today? Will you talk to the camera?'

'But of course!' her whole appearance had also changed after eating. Her face looked plumper.

'Ok, let's go. Where do we do this?' asked Carlos.

'Hold your horses!' shrieked Sara suddenly, 'You don't think for a minute you're going to interview me looking LIKE THIS, do you?'

Carlos and I must have looked confused.

'I have to get ready. Make myself beautiful. OR WHAT?'

I remember looking around and wondering how on earth was she going to make herself beautiful in this environment.

'Ok, first of all I need to wash my face'

'All right,' I said, still skeptical of any possibilities of personal hygiene.

In one easy swoop, Sara lifted the steaming large black can off the fire grid and carried it away from the group. Carlos and I followed her from behind with the camera. She set it on a block of concrete by one of the trucks and pulled a bar of soap out of her pocket. I noticed she had what looked like a piece of towel over her shoulder. She rearranged her hair inside a white woolen cap and bending over the can, plunged her hands into the water and splashed her face. Then she lathered the bar of soap in her hands and covered her face in white foam. A cloud of steam enveloped her in a soft haze as she kept splashing water to rinse her face. The fresh smell of the soap—it might have been just Ivory or Pears— filled our nostrils. I watched the tiny iridescent bubbles on her face and hands bursting in the cold air. It suddenly felt such a luxury to be able to wash one's face with hot water in a place like this.

'I *loooove* water. Sometimes, I get inside these trucks with a bucket of hot water and I give myself great baths. But it's always damn freezing!'

said Sara with a short laugh.

'How long have you been living here, Sara?' Carlos asked.

While she dried her face, she started giving us her story. She had been living in *The Salt Mines* for around six months. Before that, she lived in the Bronx with her husband, but got thrown into prison for a year and when she was released everything had disappeared. I wanted to ask her about the *husband*, but then remembered that Latino drag queens always talked about *maridos* or husbands whenever they had any kind of relationship with a guy, so I decided not to distract her and let her tell concentrate on her story about coming to the U.S.

Back at the bonfire, Sara disappeared for a few moments and came back wearing a thick wool white and grey turtle neck sweater. I noticed she had an empty Budweiser beer can in one hand and an army knife in the other. She cut the can with the knife into a small receptacle that she placed on the grid over the fire. She produced what looked like a small bar of yellow soap from a plastic bag and placed it carefully inside the Budweiser can. Suddenly, I understood what this mysterious looking ritual was about.

'Sara! You're not going to wax your legs right now!' I exclaimed.

She gave me an amused look.

'Not my legs, girl, my face. How else do I look impeccably beautiful for the camera?'

She laid out a large piece of broken mirror and all kinds of beauty aids on one of the crates. When the wax was crackling, she removed it carefully from the fire. She sat down, propped up the mirror and leaning close to it, started applying the melted wax on the surface of her cheeks and chin. Carlos had started the camera on her and the rest of the group dropped their conversation and gathered around the waxing scene, watching intently every one of her moves and laughing at her theatrical little ouches every time she pealed the yellow strips off her cheeks and upper lip. When she finished up, she rubbed skin tonic all over her red blotchy face.

'Done. No more ugly hairs poking around,' she said with satisfaction. 'I used to have quite a beard, you know?'

The ritual continued. Eyebrow plucking, face cream and foundation, eyeliner and mascara on eyes and lashes. She worked fast, every stroke perfect. I was amazed at her level of skill. She looked like a professional make-up person. Finally, she pulled off her hat and brushed her hair vigorously into a shining blond mane. The whole group watched on, fascinated by her alchemical transformation from a squalid transvestite into a sensational diva. I tried to shake myself out of the spell and jumpstart the interview.

'Sara, tell me how you came to the United States,' I asked her.

She was silent for a beat while she looked thoughtfully into the mirror making finishing touches. Then, looking at me briefly, she wiped her nose with the back of her hand, and returning to the mirror, started telling her story.

She had come from Cuba with the Mariel boatlift in 1980, a Cuban exodus by sea arranged by Fidel Castro and President Jimmy Carter that brought over a hundred and twenty five thousand Cubans into the United States. The operation had turned sour when it had come to light that some of the Cuban exiles had been released from prison and mental health institutions.

'Why did you want to come to the U.S.?'

'WHY? My God! For me the United States was the most marvelous place on earth, where you could have anything you wanted, ANYTHING! But now that I'm here, I see things differently, and I would back to Cuba any day, even to prison, 'cause here, if you have no money, you have nothing.'

She was sitting on a concrete structure close to one of the abandoned buildings, away from the fire and the bustle of the group. The
cold was unbearable. I wondered how much time we had to interview
her before she froze. The afternoon was quickly waning and we would
soon have to start dealing with dimming light. We didn't have much
time. I also knew this was probably the only time we would get Sara to
talk to us on camera.

Twilight surrounded her like a halo. It was the magic hour, the last
hour of sunlight in the day, with soft reddish light and long shadows.
The freezing air was already working through the layers of make-up
bringing up raw pink skin in the rims around her nostrils and eyelids.
It added vulnerability to her beauty.

'But of course,' she added after a beat, 'Here there is freedom. And
freedom is the one awesome thing about this country. A gay person
can *never* be happy in Cuba. They were always bothering me. Once I
got arrested because I colored my hair. I dyed it red. They shaved my
head and left me looking like a billiard ball.' She tried to laugh, but
something choked in her throat.

I tried to shake off the emotion that was also taking hold of me.
Time was more of a pressing factor than ever; I knew we could hardly
count on five to seven minutes of light. Sara was hugging her arms
across her chest now. It was freezing. I thought of Carlos's bare hands
operating the cold camera. We needed to turn a corner. Fast.

'So, were you dressing as a woman in Cuba?'

She laughed.

'NO WAY! I started dressing after I came to New York'

'Tell me about it.'

Her eyes brightened.

'I met a transvestite, and she said, "You are so beautiful, you need to start dressing." I was ashamed, but she gave me hormones, "Once you take these, you will feel the desire to dress like a woman." And that's what happened'

I wanted to stop her right there and ask her to elaborate more on this. But Sara was already running.

'The first night I went to the street dressed as Sara, a couple came to me immediately, a beautiful black man with a white woman—I went off with them. Then another guy came around, then another, and another. When I got home late that night I counted my money. I had made five hundred dollars! I looked at myself in the mirror and I cried, "I am a woman! I'm staying like this!"

She was throwing her arms around as if tossing a huge pile of dollar bills in the air.

'I couldn't believe what I had accomplished that day!'

For a moment, I stood swept up in the images her story was arousing in my imagination. The limelight in the night street, the glitter of the unprecedented money pile. Their magic pulled you away from the garbage and the struggle against the ever encroaching cold.

Carlos said, 'We have to stop shooting. All the batteries are spent. I would need to go back to the fire for a fresh one.'

There was no time for that. The sun was rapidly sinking and Sara was shivering. That was it for the day.

As we approached Gigi, Edwin and Ruben sitting around the fire, another thought was taking hold of me. Carlos had left equipment by the fire? Wasn't he worried it would disappear? I saw him sit down close to Gigi, set down the camera at his feet and ask her for the production bag. Gigi reached over to her side, pulled it up and handed it over to him. It was a big dark blue production bag where we kept tapes, extra batteries, a microphone and a Sun Gun. It was bulky and heavy to carry around, but I was surprised that he would be trusting Gigi with hundreds of dollars' worth of equipment while we were shooting somewhere else. I suddenly realized how comfortable we were beginning to feel in *The Salt Mines*, how closely bonded we were with some of its inhabitants.

Sara was leaving.

'Sorry guys, but I have a date tonight,' she said with a mischievous look putting on her camel coat and some gloves.

'A date?' Ruben and Gigi snickered.

'Sara, I need to film you in the street at night.'

'UUUUHH!' cooed Ruben.

'All right,' said Sara, 'When?'

'Tomorrow.'

'Tomorrow is Monday. Not good. Thursday'

'Deal.'

She disappeared into the darkness.

We were exhausted but the scene that remained was impossible not to film. Finally, Gigi and Edwin together after months separated by bars. We decided to stay, and started setting up the equipment to film again. Edwin and Gigi were drinking out of some can the label of which I couldn't distinguish in the dim light. I assumed it was beer, but later found out that Edwin only drank soda. They were teasing one another in a flirty way.

'Today was my birthday and you didn't even bring me flowers,' Gigi was saying.

'You didn't even greet me when I arrived,' Edwin retorted, 'You said, I'm high don't even look at me.'

'I had to get high to bear the excitement of getting you back!' Gigi said. Then she clicked her tongue and added with a laugh, 'You men are all the same!'

Edwin came over to her crate and embraced her. They stood cheek to cheek, gazing at the dying flames exhaling glowing sparks into the night air. I could feel the warmth of their togetherness, their drunk-happy dreamy eyes. I remembered Gigi's words about how her love with Edwin was the deepest, strongest bond in the world.

Meanwhile, Ruben was leaning over his broken chair and playing with a doll he had presumably found in the trash. It was a pink blonde toddler doll on all fours with a big pacifier in her mouth. Ruben had wound her up and it was moving its little hands and knees trying to crawl with a broken whizzing sound. Ruben kept pushing her softly along while listening to Edwin and Gigi talk, a placid smile on his face. There was a feeling of peace in the air, as if the pressure of time and life's tribulations had been suspended in the most tender moment we were ever to witness in *The Salt Mines*.

'Tell me about prison,' I said to Edwin.

He shrugged his shoulders while his face broke into a lazy smile. There was a childlike quality to Edwin that made him instantly endearing. He was probably very young, no older that twenty or twenty one.

'He can't tell you anything,' jumped in Gigi, 'The cat got his tongue. He's in shock of coming back to me after all this time,' she teased. Edwin punched her playfully in revenge.

'Okay, you tell me about going to prison as a drag queen then,' I said to Gigi.

'Well, that is THE biggest scandal!' said Gigi. She was smiling seductively at Edwin and I knew that whatever tale she was going to come up with, it was for Edwin and not for us. The camera, Carlos and I were just props in the theatrical display she was about to perform for her lover.

Then Carlos said, 'We're out of batteries. We can't shoot anymore.'

'Out of batteries?' I protested, 'I thought you had extra ones in the bag.'

'Nope. They're all dead by now.'

Something inside me crashed. How frustrating could this be? We were all warmed up to shoot an amazing scene and the technical side of things was refusing to cooperate. My first reaction was to feel fury at myself, or even at Carlos, for not anticipating a situation like this, for not bringing double amount of tapes, batteries or of the whole gamut of production gear items. Then, I remembered we had been shooting for over four hours and that we were, after all, a miracle skeleton crew of two, who already handled an incredibly complex situation. I relaxed somewhat, but the taste of failure remained in my mouth. Carlos put the camera down between his feet. I knew he was exhausted.

However, Gigi was not concerned in the least with this production drawback; it didn't interfere at all with her agenda. She was coming into her full blown stage persona. She ran her fingers through her hair as if to reorganize a great hairdo.

'Drag queens don't have it bad in prison at all. First of all, it is FULL of men, and of course, with VERY little or NO competition at all. The very first day the guards take you down the gallery to your cell it's just like going on the catwalk with all the prisoners cheering and banging on the bars, because even if they're calling you *maricón* and faggot, you know they're looking at your ass. You know they're hoping you can be their girl.'

'Do you mean gay inmates?' I asked.

'It depends what you call *gay inmates*,' Gigi laughed, 'Out here they might not be gay, but in there, many of them become *bujarrones*, or buggers, if they get an opportunity'. She turned to stare at Edwin who was listening intently.

'So then, the problem becomes what to do with all these *bujarrones* slobbering all over you. When you walk into the dining room, everyone wants to sit with you, everyone wants to bring your tray over for you. When you go take a shower, guards have to clear the bathrooms and stand at the door while you wash. Phew, it can get VERY crowded!' she said fanning her face with her hand in a comical gesture. I could see how the performance was already making Edwin uneasy. He was standing with his hands in the pockets of his leather jacket, looking at his feet.

'Then all sorts of fights start breaking up about you. And although it's flattering, it can get you in trouble. The guards realize you're dynamite and they decide to put you in solitary confinement to avoid a mutiny.'

I wanted to laugh at the word 'mutiny'. But, hey, what did I know about prisons and their dynamics? It could all be true. I stole a glance at Carlos and saw a big grin on his face. I knew he was also enjoying the show.

'So there is only one solution,' Gigi continued, 'You look for the strongest, the most powerful guy in the joint and you become his woman. And he will keep everyone else at bay, get you goodies and pamper you to no end. And then, YOU'RE SET!'

She looked at us, self-satisfied and exuberant, and then added with her raspy laugh, 'Hopefully, the guy is also good looking and sexy!'

Although her acting was flawless, I knew she was watching Edwin closely from the corner of her eye. Edwin had taken a step back and was standing rigidly with his eyes fixed on the fire. Again I wondered if it was all just a fantasy tale to make Edwin insanely jealous.

'What an amazing story. Is it really true?' I couldn't help blurting out.

Gigi nodded smilingly and arched her eyebrows with silent pride.

'It *is* true' confirmed Ruben who had been listening in fascination all this time, 'Every drag queen who goes to the joint says the same thing.'

There was a moment of silence while I became—or maybe we all did—painfully aware of Edwin. Gigi must have picked it up, or decided she had punished him enough, because she said, 'But those are things a girl does to survive in the joint. They never change your real heart. I think of Edwin every single moment and count the days when I will see him again,' she reached towards Edwin, but he brushed her off. She laughed and threw her arms around him pawing him until he finally yielded.

I was totally absorbed in this scene when suddenly something scurried around my feet and I jumped up. 'Shit! What was that?'

'Oh, it's probably a rat or something,' said Ruben without looking up.

I froze. I'm not particularly afraid of rats, but having them run at my feet was a very different matter. In an instant I was struck with a very clear vision of an obvious reality. *The Salt Mines* was swarming with rats and all kinds of other critters. How could it not be? And how come I hadn't realized before?

I was still standing when Carlos said, 'Hell, look at them over there!'

To my left I saw two huge rats in the dark carrying away the remnants of the hamburger meat that had been left in the brown wrapping paper. They disappeared with their booty underneath the closest truck.

Carlos said, 'Are you all right? Come and sit by me over here.'

I sat next to him shivering.

'How come we haven't seen them before? I guess they're all over the place,' I said to Carlos.

'They don't show their face because of the cold,' said Gigi.

'Yeah, they stay in the trucks,' said Edwin.

'They stay close to us when we sleep so they can get our body heat,' laughed Gigi.

I was horrified and I thought they were joking.

'Aren't you afraid they will bite you or something?' I asked.

'Nah,' replied Edwin, 'Not if you don't bother them. They just want to be left alone. I can tell you they're better roommates than some of those prison asses.'

This was our chance of getting Edwin to talk about his experience in prison. But I had had enough for one day. I needed to leave.

Back in the apartment I rushed into the bathroom as soon as we lay down the equipment and got under the hottest shower I could run. I scrubbed my body thoroughly and washed my hair twice, brushed my teeth—obsessively engaging in every bit of cleaning endeavor I could think of. I couldn't get enough of the soap and the smell of water. After emerging from the bathroom, reddened and engorged with the scalding water, I put all the clothes I had been wearing that day inside a garbage bag, including my coat and boots. Tomorrow I would take it all to the laundry and wash it thoroughly and the coat would be hung by the fire escape together with the boots, and sprayed with Lysol. Those rats had pierced me to the bone. Realistically, how long could I keep going down to *The Salt Mines*?

However, that night I had walked away from *The Salt Mines* with one obsessive thought in my head. We had to film these guys working in the streets at night. We couldn't just stay in the sanitation enclosure with them, we needed to get a glimpse at them interacting with the rest of the world. This was not easy. They were prostitutes who worked in the Meatpacking district on 14th Street, a gloomy area lined with large brick buildings along dark cobbled streets adjacent to *The Salt Mines*. Back then, this part of town was very different to what it has come to be today, a hip neighborhood with high end shops, expensive restaurants and galleries swarming with tourists and classy New Yorkers. It was a real meat market with somber buildings and warehouses made to look even darker by long metal canopies covering the sidewalks, under which hung strange elaborate rails with lines of enormous hooks. During the day, the district was full of gigantic trucks unloading carcasses of cattle, raw pink and red pieces beheaded, behooved and peeled away from hide and skin, that stood in the street hanging and bleeding from those hooks waiting to get wheeled inside the warehouses. After six or seven o'clock, when business hours were over for the meat packers, the district became a murky empty area where dry blood still covered the cobble stones and the smell of dead meat lingered heavily. Then, a whole new scene emerged: a swarm of prostitutes, pimps and those seeking their services invaded the dark streets. It was, as Gigi said, a true meat market around the clock, *during the day it is beef, at night it is human meat.*

I wasn't sure how we would film in a place like this. If we just walked around with a camera we would probably scare the whole scene away or just get harassed. Prostitution is very secretive, even more if you are looking for a male hustler or a drag queen. We didn't just want to interview drag queens on location, we wanted to capture the space with its comings and goings. We really needed a car that could drive us around from where we could shoot unseen. It could also capture the feeling of searching for a prostitute from the client's point of view, since most of them drove around looking for someone to pick up.

Carlos and I had only one friend with a car. His name was Xavier. He was a pathologist who had become bored with the medical world and was interested in art projects that explored the darker side of the city. I called him and asked him if he would lend his car and act as a chauffeur driving us around and he agreed. We had a car for the shoot.

There was also another question. Sara had found out I had given clothes to Giovanna and asked me if I had any more. I didn't, but I could go about collecting some more. This time I wanted something special because I knew that's what Sara would probably be wearing for the night shoot. I didn't think about it then, but in retrospect I was violating one of the golden rules of documentary: never interfere with the reality you are shooting. My first donation of clothes to Giovanna had been just that, a donation for the purpose of helping out a group of homeless people who were cold. Although of course there was the intention of creating trust and bonding with them. This time around, though, the clothes would definitively influence the sequence of events we were about to shoot.

But I only learned this later. For the time being, I decided to call my friend Gabriella. She was a beautiful Peruvian actress who always seemed to have extra clothes and accessories and gave me the things she didn't wear anymore. I went to see her and told her about Sara.

She said, 'I was keeping a coat for you. But if you want to use it for the shoot, go ahead. Nothing like a good prop to enhance a scene.'

She was in the film and theater world and of course the words 'scene' and 'prop' spelled fiction. And they might have made me reflect on the fact that I was designing a scene instead of just capturing a raw reality. But I didn't see it that way then. I was just in love with the idea of shooting a beautiful drag queen working the streets in the downtown night.

The coat was awesome. It was a light gray faux with a cottony look and feel. It was secondhand, but in great condition. I don't know where she might have gotten it from. She was a struggling actress working as a waitress while she hunted down the city for auditions. And although frequently broke like the rest of us, she was always dressed to the nines in a very effective combination of chic feminine and scruffy downtown elements. Heads turned in the street when she walked by.

My case was different. My presentation to the world as a filmmaker required a more masculine attire. Jeans, boots, short coats or jackets that would allow you to handle and haul equipment or to move quickly in any given situation. Not that I didn't own one or two party dresses, but the day-to-day was practical gear. My meager financial resources at the time didn't even allow me all the clothes I really needed for shooting in a situation like *The Salt Mines*. Ideally, Carlos and I should have bought ski or high mountain gear, but that would have been a fortune. Instead we had to pile sweaters under our coats and socks inside our boots. But it was never enough. After a few of hours filming in the open, no matter what we did, we would begin to freeze and had to abandon the shoot.

I took the coat in my hands. It felt warm and fuzzy and I loved the color. It wasn't a coat I would have been able to afford even in a second-hand shop. And I didn't have a good coat at the time, just a small collection of shabby leather jackets. This coat was long, it went below the knees, and it had a collar that could be buttoned right up to the chin. So perfect for New York winters.

I folded it and put it away in the bag with a pang. I couldn't afford to get attached to it. It *had* to go towards the shoot.

Gabriella must have perceived my regret, because she said consolingly, 'Oh, don't worry. You can always send it to the cleaners after the shoot.'

But she didn't understand that I would never see this coat again after the shoot. It would very likely be swallowed up into the night together with Sara. And it would either get stolen, traded for crack, or just lost. It was one of those one-time props. I thanked her and left.

When I got home I saw she had included a bunch of other accessories in the bag. Black lace pantyhose, a cheap but beautiful long string of pearls, an old longish black dress. A complete outfit.

Thursday came. I was so nervous I could have screamed all day long. I had to wait for the night and for Xavier and Carlos to get out of work. I checked on the video equipment, batteries, tapes, microphones—everything I could think of—a number of times. I looked at the clothes, too. I couldn't do anything else and couldn't stay put. My worse fear of course was that Sara wouldn't show up. It had been so difficult to find her in *The Salt Mines*. Why would she keep her word this time or even remember about it today? It was so easy for the crazy current of her life to pull her adrift towards any other shore. Years later, I still marvel that Sara actually did turn up that night. Maybe she was not as wild-minded and out of control as she appeared to be, or maybe she had become hooked to the documentary after we interviewed her on camera. She had succumbed to the addictive power of telling your story through a lens. That way, she wasn't much different to millions of other human beings.

It was nearly eight o'clock when Xavier rang the doorbell of our apartment announcing he was parked downstairs. We lugged the equipment downstairs and got into the car. But it was too early. Sara had told us that no real hustling would start until after ten. We had to kill time.

We decided to go down to the Meatpacking District and explore our location. I had done a little of this by foot but only during the daytime. It was a lonely and possibly dangerous place to walk in during the night. Now I realized that more preproduction time should have been employed in mapping out the district and choosing points for specific shots, but it was too late. Everything was in motion at this point and there was no going back. We drove around the deserted streets for a while. Carlos had rolled down the window and was setting up the camera to shoot from the copilot seat. I was getting ready to hold a shotgun microphone out of the window on the back. The streets were cobbled, which meant that no matter how slow the ride, it would feel very bumpy and reflect on the stability of the shot. We instructed Xavier to drive extremely slowly, and went around a couple of blocks before he could understand that he literally had to crawl more than drive. The time was approaching for our appointment with Sara.

We parked the car on 13th Street and Washington Street where we had agreed to meet her. As soon as I stepped out of the car, I got hit by the fierce wind. This was a point where winds blowing down opposite avenues met and lashed at each other. Anyone caught in the intersection got lacerated by their icy whips. I saw the tight group approaching the corner almost instantly. I recognized Sara, but not the other two that came with her. I was hoping Giovanna and Gigi would be with her, but instead she had brought two new drag queens along. One was a thickset transvestite with shoulder length hair, wearing a short skirt and bright red leggings. The other one was a lanky boyish-looking queen with a thin blue coat over a pink dress with a very low neckline. They both looked excited to meet me. Sara was wearing a shiny lamé dress under her camel coat and pointed high heel shoes.

Sara saw my hesitation about her friends.

'They don't need to come with us,' she said gesturing towards them.

But I saw they were all shivering, like me.

'Well, we have a bunch of coffee in the car.'

'We don't all fit in the car,' snapped Sara, and turning to them she said, 'Sorry girls, we'll have to meet up later.'

There was a harshness to her voice. I thought she might not want to share us or let anyone steal the limelight of the situation. They left without a word. We got into the car's back seat. I introduced Sara to Xavier.

She said, 'Enchanté,' and batted her eyelids while she extended a hand to him. I saw that she had done her nails for the occasion. Her makeup was also flashy with thick eyeliner and red lips. But sitting this close to her I was perceiving the pungent smell of dirt coming from her clothes and body. It was the smell of homelessness, that mixture of grime with strong undertones of rot and urine. The warm contained space of the car had the effect of magnifying it, as it unfolded into deeper layers of stench that invaded every cavity of the nose. I suppressed and instinctive wince. I reflected that the chilled air of *The Salt Mines* I constantly moaned about had the one advantage of keeping these odors at bay.

I showed her the coat and she shrieked.

'OH, MY GOD! This is a die for!'

Then I showed her the lace pantyhose and the dress, and she shrieked some more. Carlos and Xavier watched the scene in fascination from the front seat.

Then Sara said, 'Okay boys, turn around. I'm going to put on some stockings,' and she started wriggling into the pantyhose against the narrow back seat. After she had pulled them up to her waist, she considered the dress, but decided it was too slim for her. She put on the string of pearls and the coat. And turning around towards me, she said. 'Tell me I look like a million dollars. TONIGHT I'M GOING FOR THE TOTAL KILL!'

Carlos and Xavier whisked around and dropped their mouths dramatically to humor her. But the truth was she *did* look dressed to kill.

I offered her a cup of coffee. She took a couple of sips, but she was too excited to stay inside the car. She couldn't wait to start the hunt. When she stepped out, I rolled down the window and said, 'We're going to follow you, all right? So walk close to the lighted areas and remember we have to drive slowly.'

She nodded but I could see her eyes already scanning the dark streets nervously ahead of her. Later I learned that she was probably experiencing what crack users call *thirst*, that is, the irresistible anticipation of the moment when they will consume the drug.

She suddenly darted away from the car calling out some name that I didn't quite get. When I yelled after her, she just said, 'I'll find you later!' And disappeared.

We hadn't anticipated this. We were going to have to hunt Sara down in the meat district.

We started cruising through the murky avenues. The blocks were very long and poorly lit. The street lights threw dark yellow shafts on the facades of buildings, but the rest of the street remained pitch black. In some areas the car headlights were the only source of light. The narrow streets seemed to be devoid of all human element at first, although we soon started making out certain shadows standing in corners and alleys. I asked Carlos to film everything he could from the car window.

'You're not going to be able to see anything in this light,' he said.

'Can't you bring up the gain?' I asked.

Gain is a camera mode in which low light images are enhanced in video, making them look very grainy, but at least allowing you to capture something.

'You think of gain as a magical wand,' Carlos said. I could feel in his voice that he also was upset at Sara's disappearance and the possibility of not being able to film.

'Please!' I begged. I could feel frustration tightening my chest.

I don't know what I was begging for. I knew gain could only save the day occasionally, hardly under this degree of darkness. Carlos knew his stuff.

But he actually turned on the gain and said, 'OK. Let's just shoot and we'll see what turns out. Nothing to lose at this point, I suppose.'

We all grew silent in the car. I looked at my watch. It was just past eleven. I started noticing that either my eyes were adjusting to the dark, or the night activity was beginning to stir. Suddenly, there were silhouettes moving under the gloomy canopies and brick thresholds of buildings. As the car swept by, a glint of flesh might spark up in the dark, a pair of thighs or bare breasts, a masked face with pouting lips, and then fade away quickly. As we turned a corner we saw a phantom-like figure coming towards us, her half-naked body gleaming in a gray pearly hue. She was wearing high platform shoes with exposed garters holding stockings over thin bony legs. She moved affectedly in slow motion.

'Stop. Stop the car!' I said to Xavier. 'Let's ask her about Sara.'

Xavier stopped and the creature floated towards us while I rolled down the window.

'Do you know where I can find a queen called Sara?'

She thrust her head towards the window to scan the inside of the car. I observed her extreme youth under the heavy makeup and red-painted hair.

She then looked me in the eye with infinite scorn and said, 'Sorry, I don't do women–'

'No, no,' I said, 'I'm just looking for–'

'I don't know Sara either,' she interrupted. 'All I know is Candy. That's me,' she said theatrically, pointing a long finger to her chest. She swirled around and walked back into the shadows.

I was pissed, but Xavier found it really funny.

'I'm beginning to get the knack of this—I can see how it could get real interesting,' he joked.

We continued to drive around. There was a fascination to this labyrinth of dark corridors where strange characters suddenly popped up for an instant and then disappeared without a trace. As the night advanced, more hustlers were openly showing themselves on sidewalks and corners. Some were in drag and others were just slender boy hustlers. More cars were driving around, too.

'Hungry sharks foraging for prey,' mused Xavier from behind the wheel.

The cars parked in obscure deserted spots and waited for a hustler to step out of the dark, approach them and start negotiating. Then they would either close the deal and get into the car, or move swiftly away. Sometimes the haggling got intense, and the hustler would come and go a couple of times from the street to the car shrieking things like, "No way!" and "Up yours, faggot!" However, even after hot-headed exchanges, most deals were struck.

But Sara was still missing.

I was thinking of stepping out of the car and talking another drag queen into filming. At least we would walk away with something. But it would be difficult to tie it back to the characters we already had on tape from *The Salt Mines*. It might end up being just a general scene of hustling, or introduce a new character that would take us down a different road. Documentaries can do that. They can start you off with one reality, and then take you on unforeseen journeys. This is the beauty and the danger. I was thinking about all this, and then considered an additional factor. There was no way I could pull off a shoot with an unknown hustler without paying out some money. The scene out here was too hot right now for these guys to be generous with their time. I would have to compensate their losing business with something. And how much would that be? Twenty, forty? How much did I have in my pocket right now?

'Hey! There she is!' said Xavier.

At the far end of the avenue I recognized the beautiful gray coat under the yellowish light of a street lamp. Sara was holding onto the lamp post with one hand in a theatrical gesture, her head thrown back and her slim body slithering under the open coat. She might have been singing one of her cabaret songs.

'Let's get to her. Quick. Before she disappears again,' I said.

I wanted Xavier to step on the gas. I feared the worst, that she might already be wasted.

I got out of the car.

'Sara—'

'Hey, where were YOU?' she said.

There was a dreamy look over her face but when I looked into her eyes, I saw a hardness in her pupil that I had never seen before. Like an impenetrable black hunger, a texture one imagines in eyes hidden behind ancient Aztec masks or African statues. For a moment, I felt frightened.

She pulled her eyes away from mine and circled the street lamp again. I could feel the tension in her movements.

'I have been VERY busy. And done VERY well. Already over three tricks. This is a glorious night!' she spoke quickly and excitedly.

'Oh, there's another one coming right up. I need to go. See you later!'

She was already stepping towards an approaching car.

'Sara, we had a deal,' I said, 'We were going to film you tonight.'

'We can always do that later. I need to take this guy.'

I reached out and touched her wrist. Her whole body cringed and the hard look came into her eyes again. I was about to regret having touched her, but then she turned. I saw a struggle twitching in her face.

'You're right. If I take another hit, it'll be the end of the production.'

Something relaxed in her glance, like an instant sobering up. She waved away the trick in the car.

'What do you want me to do?'

'I want you to pick up another trick for the camera'

'ALL RIGHT! Let's go!'

I went back to the car.

'Can we do a shot following her from behind?'

Sara graciously waited until we had the camera equipment ready. She put on more lipstick and pampered her hair.

'Just walk along as if you're looking for clients,' I said.

'Only that there's no way I'm going to get hit on if they see that big bad camera behind me,' she was back to her joking self.

'All right, we'll follow you for a while, then hide and film you falling on your prey.'

'Sounds like a great plan, specially the falling part. A total SCANDAL!' she pealed.

And she started giving us *the* walk, swaying her hips arms akimbo under the open coat and clip clopping her high heels on the cobbled road. Carlos followed her, handholding the camera. Despite the technical retinue, she started getting cat calls from all the vehicles that drove by.

'I think we need to retreat into the car. Something is going to happen soon and I want to make sure we get it,' I whispered into Carlos's ear.

Sure enough, we were hardly back inside the car when a minivan stopped at Sara's side. The scene was quickly unfolding at the back of our car and I was in a sudden panic as how to shoot it without being noticed. Then I saw that Carlos was already shooting the scene through the side mirror. Discreet and totally brilliant! In the beginning there was some going back and forth between Sara and the hidden minivan driver but a minute later she got into the car. Done deal. The minivan drove off.

Hey! I didn't know you were such a good producer. You handled things incredibly well out there,' said Xavier, sipping coffee at an all-night deli after the shoot. I looked at him in disbelief and then considered he knew very little about producing and directing documentaries. But on second thought, I reflected that even factoring in my mistakes, I hadn't done a bad job after all. We had succeeded in shooting a segment in difficult conditions, and I had pulled many strings in order to bring it together. I hadn't lost my nerve when things had become uncertain with Sara. I had been constantly racking my brain in case a plan B was needed. For the first time I saw how I was maturing as a producer.

However, months later in the editing room when I looked again at the footage we shot that night, I realized that, despite my rich memories of the shoot, we had only succeeded in capturing a bunch of dark moving shots with a few flashes of light here and there, and the few more elaborate shots of Sara. It was enough to create a short sequence evocative of a hustling scene, but not much more. I edited the shots together in a slow motion sequence. Even though the car had crawled through the streets, the shots had to be slowed down even further for the viewer to appreciate the images. It ended up looking like a nightmarish scene, with a floating dreamy pace. A journey through a labyrinth of purgatory or hell.

Later, when we talked to Elliot Sharp, the musician who composed the music for the final documentary, of all the scenes in the film, he had most questions about this sequence. He wanted to know what type of track he should compose for it, what kind of feeling it should suggest to the viewer. He sounded like he was having a hard time chewing on the sequence. We really liked Elliot's compositions and we wanted him to come up with his own ideas for the piece.

So we said to him, 'Imagine you go down there looking for a drag queen to satisfy an urge. Just play it from there.'

And the music he came up with captured all that, the eerie quality of the darkness, the morbid secrecy of the hunt and the mounting excitement as Sara steps into the scene and is picked up by a trick.

The Sunday following the night shoot we decided to go down to *The Salt Mines* again. The night shoot had given us a deeper glimpse into the Salt Queens' lives and I wanted to build on it, although I wasn't quite sure how. It had been raining hard for the last two days and the day was overcast and chilly with wicked gusts of wind. After we left the apartment with the equipment and just before we hailed a cab, I decided to get some extra food to take down. I snuck into a Cuban diner just a few blocks down on Eight Avenue and ordered two roasted chickens to go. As I was waiting at the counter for the guy to wrap them up, I reflected on the fact that we had been taking increasing amounts food and drinks down to *The Salt Mines* as time went on. I had even added an extra backpack to our equipment just for food alone.

Both Carlos and I sat in the back of the taxi in silence while it whizzed down towards the piers below 14th Street unhindered by the usual weekday traffic jams. I was thinking how to get them to talk about their experiences as prostitutes. How did they cope with strange men who they would never probably see again? Was it all just the money and the drugs, or was there something else in that exchange, some other thrill, such as an irresistible desire to step into the unknown?

When we arrived at *The Salt Mines* we heard loud voices coming from the trucks as if there might be a brawl or a loud argument. We plodded over the soaked garbage, worried that we might find a situation with unknown people who wouldn't be happy to see a video crew. But as we approached the opening with the yellow sofa and the crates we saw there were no new players, only a new type of scene. Gigi and Giovanna stood confronting each other over the smoldering remains of a dying fire. They were screaming into each other's faces. Both looked dirty and spent, their hair dishevelled and their clothes dingier than ever. Around them sat Sara, Ruben and Michael listening idly to their dispute. From the corner of my eye I saw Carlos quickly swing the camera onto his shoulder and begin to shoot the scene.

'You never gave me my part of the clothes, you faggot!' screamed Gigi.

'Yes, I did,' Giovanna screamed back, 'I gave you the sweater you're wearing right now!'

'You were supposed to give me half of the lot!' Gigi's voice was hoarse and threatening.

'Nothing here belongs to anyone!' pealed Giovanna in a shrill voice.

'I'm going to give it to you, faggot, *cabrón!*' Gigi was advancing menacingly towards her.

'There's no private property here,' Giovanna's voice was getting more and more shrill as Gigi's voice was getting deeper. And in fact, Gigi was acting the most masculine I had ever seen her, while Giovanna was looking more and more like a hysterical queen.

It took me a few minutes to figure out what the discussion was about, but suddenly it hit me. The clothes I had given Giovanna! She hadn't shared them with Gigi, although I had specifically asked her to. Gigi had found out and she was mad. She probably also found out about the coat and accessories I had given Sara for the night shoot on Thursday. I felt terrible. This was all my fault. How had I not thought about Gigi? Why had I taken for granted that Giovanna would share? It was another example of the rippling effects of meddling with the reality you are filming. For a second I forgot myself and stepped towards them with the intention of breaking up the fight and explaining it was all my fault and I would make amends by bringing more clothes.

But Carlos extended his left arm barring me from moving towards them. My intervention was not going to break up the fight and this was, in fact, a great scene to film.

'I'm gonna hit you, *cabrón*,' Gigi lunged towards Giovanna. She used classical Spanish masculine names to insult her, like *maricón* or faggot and also *cabrón*, son of a bitch or literally, *cuckold*. Sara suddenly stood up, walked towards Gigi and took her by the arm, whispering a few words into her ear which I didn't get to hear. Gigi paid no attention and kept going at Giovanna.

'We're going to have it out you and I!'

Sara started pulling her more forcibly away from the circle.

'Let go off her Gigi. Let's go get something to eat,' she said.

Gigi eventually yielded and let herself be pulled away but kept turning her head now and then, muttering, 'I'm gonna hit you, *cabrón*.'

Carlos and I followed Gigi and Sara with the camera as they walked away from the trucks towards the gate. Sara had threaded her arm through Gigi's and was walking very close to her, comforting her with words. Before they turned a corner, Sara looked back at us as her face opened wide into an amused smile. She was truly delighted by the whole happening, fight, camera and all. At one point she made Gigi turn towards us and she took her face with her hands and kissed her on the lips. Then she looked back at us, broke into laughter and taking Gigi's arm once more, walked away swaying her hips.

Back at the circle, Giovanna, Michael and Ruben were sitting around the smoking embers. Michael was trying to stoke the flames by adding pieces of carton and a few splinters of wood. Giovanna was screaming furiously, 'The hair, that's the only thing. Because she talks like a man, walks like a man and has a body like a man!'

'No, Gigi is feminine—she is as feminine as you are,' retorted Ruben in an even tone.

'Lies!' pealed Giovanna looking at the camera with a malicious smirk.

'Every time two queens fight, SHE'S A MAN!' said Ruben laughing, 'Gigi is all cut down, she looks just like my aunt…' he added more seriously.

'You're only saying that because you like her,' said Giovanna with a huff, rearranging her hat and scarf as I had seen her do before when she had to assert herself.

'I like you too, and you look like a man,' said Ruben.

'WELL, THAT'S A LIE!' shrieked Giovanna. She got up and demonstrated a stomping swaggering walk with open legs and a hunched back.

'I DO NOT WALK LIKE THIS!' And bursting into laughter she walked back towards the fire repeating in a singsong voice,

'She walks like a man, she talks like a man, she hates like a man… She probably fights like a man too!' She sat down on a crate and huddled into her dirty green coat shuddering. Then she looked up and her face was gaunt with eyes and nose running from the freezing air.

'She's always confronting everyone,' she said.

'Everyone confronts everyone,' responded Ruben, 'I've confronted you, and you me, and you've confronted Gigi, and Sara and so on,' he continued. I was suddenly struck with the authority with which Ruben was handling the situation. Like a seasoned mediator between two old enemies. It was amazing how this kid, probably not even sixteen, who was always hanging around in the role of apprentice or understudy of these older and seemingly more experienced drag queens, could suddenly come up with opinions and postulations that settled arguments.

'How can we survive in a place like this if we don't do that?' Giovanna said after a moment. Her voice was hollow with an immense sadness.

The wind had picked up and was blowing straight from the river. We were all shivering. Giovanna looked around the fire despairingly.

'Please Michael, bring over that piece of wood so we can burn it. It's sooo freezing!' She was trembling visibly.

Michael objected raising his eyebrows over smiling eyes.

'Me? Why me?' he said jokingly and Giovanna gave him an imploring look. Then he got up laughing softly and walked over to the piece of wood.

For some reason, I too was shaken after this scene. I remember resisting the idea of leaving *The Salt Mines* that day. How could I go back home to my cozy little apartment and leave them all here with this unbearable cold and miserable sadness? My apartment suddenly felt like a luxurious palace with actual walls and windows overlooking a small garden, with running water, a gas cooker, a fridge, and a soft clean bed. A jeweled collection of bright colors compared to the ever gray landscape of *The Salt Mines*. The more I kept going down to *The Salt Mines*, the more amazingly appreciative I became of the comforts and few belongings that the small precious habitat that was our apartment held. At times, I remember being conscious of feeling slight distortions in my perception as I walked in from the street and suddenly found myself observing the texture of the paint on the walls, or the shape of the crooked wood floors or just taking in the smell of water running from the kitchen tap. As if coming back from *The Salt Mines* made me look at these things for the first time.

But that day I was particularly distraught at the thought of crossing back into my comfortable life. Maybe Gigi would have said, *going back to society*. The pull was to stay back with them all and bear the brunt of the street life together. The cold, the hunger, the desolation and the inevitable brotherhood—or sisterhood—that extreme struggle for survival generated. A bond forged both in the pain and the exhilaration of being alive despite it all.

When we finally left, Carlos being the decisive force, and we were back on Eighth Avenue, I realized I had totally forgotten to bring out the roasted chickens, which were still tightly packed in my backpack. For a second I thought of running back just to deliver the chickens.

'Are you crazy?' said Carlos looking at me for the first time with serious doubts in his eyes. And then seeing I was on the verge of tears, he added in a softer tone, 'Look, even if you go back there, do you think they're still going to be around? Chances are you will find nobody.'

He was right. The image of *The Salt Mines* as a strange theater where bizarre skits suddenly flashed in and out of stage, reentered my mind. *The Salt Mines* felt suddenly like a grotesque representation of human predicament: the tortuous search for identity, the isolation from the rest of the world, the insanely difficult circumstances. It was like a distorted image of our human selves. And of course, they would no longer be there at this point. Their survival instinct would have already driven them out into the street in search of food and warmth. But, what was happening to *me*?

Only years later I would read about experiences of what they call *going native*, where anthropologists who have gone into tribal communities to study them have ended up stepping over the boundaries between the observer and the observed and getting swallowed up by the reality they intended to document from the outside. Although many accounts of *going native* were described as negative, unscientific situations, I had always admired these experiences. Suddenly the membrane between the two separate worlds was dissolved and the

Western scholar found himself not just entering, but getting lost in a totally different pocket of reality. Maybe that is what started happening to me. After a while, a part of me started living in *The Salt Mines*.

There came a point where I couldn't take the cold and the dirt anymore in our Salt Mines shoots and I fell sick. I went into a strange state of low grade fever, exhaustion and constant chills. I could not eat. It was as if the smell of filth and images of grime had invaded my lungs, throat and stomach. All I could do was lie down with closed eyes and doze under a pile of blankets. But there was no quietude for my producer brain. It kept on planning and scheming all kinds of details about the documentary.

A couple of days before I'd gotten sick, Gigi had talked about the possibility of us shooting her and a friend going uptown to buy hormones. She told us that there was a woman working in a pharmacy in East Harlem that sold them hormones under the counter. I was developing an increased fascination with the topic of hormones and transvestites, since it seemed to be the magical elixir that allowed them to cross boundaries between the masculine and the feminine realms. From the interviews we had shot with them, I had gathered that the use of hormones changed the quality of their muscle and skin, and even influenced the way they felt about their sexual identity. I was eager to portray all this in the film.

Christmas was approaching and time was more pressing than ever. I tried to talk Carlos into shooting a sequence about hormones without me. But Carlos was also exhausted and it was too much to ask him to

shoot in *The Salt Mines* all by himself. I thought of bringing in someone to go shoot with him. We had a Puerto Rican friend called Jorge.
He was a lawyer, a down to earth guy with a diehard social consciousness, and a good friend who had always helped us out with practical
legal matters. I called him and asked him if he would help Carlos with
a shoot. He agreed.

A couple of days later they went down to *The Salt Mines*. It was a
dull gray morning, the sky hung heavy over the city like an inverted
dome of lead. The weather forecast had announced it would snow
around mid-morning. Not the best day for a shoot. Carlos and Jorge
left the apartment about ten thirty, loaded with equipment and all
kinds of shooting plans. I stayed back with a heavy heart. I would have
given anything to go with them.

I waited all morning and into the afternoon for them to come back.
It started to snow around twelve, soft flurries falling steadily outside the
window, silently coating the dark fire escape into a mesh of white lace.
I was beginning to think something might have happened to them,
when I heard the key in the apartment door and in they came with
ashen faces from the cold, wet all over with melting snow. I rushed to
make tea to warm them up. They sat at the kitchen table sipping their
mugs and catching their breath.

'Well, what happened? How did it go?' I asked impatiently.

Jorge said, 'My God, what a trip!'

Apparently they had arrived at *The Salt Mines* and managed to locate
Gigi and Jennifer, the drag queen we had met days before when Gigi put
on makeup for us, and all of them had taken a trip by subway up to East
Harlem. Just traveling in the subway in the middle of the day through
midtown had already been an experience in and of itself, with Gigi and
Jenny in shabby drag Salt Mines style standing or sitting alongside men

and women in expensive corporate suits and leather briefcases going about their work day. Finally, when they had arrived in East Harlem, Gigi and Jennifer had lead the way to a small pharmacy with a beat up facade and aisles that reeked of roach powder. There they had met up with an old woman at the counter who seemed to know them, and asked her to sell them hormones. Carlos and Jorge had been instructed not to go into the pharmacy, since their presence would create suspicions and the negotiations would be blocked. They could only observe the inside scenes though the shop window from the street. There seemed to be quite a lot of haggling around with the price over the counter. Gigi started to make dramatic gestures at one point but the old woman, stood staunchly behind the counter with her arms crossed over her big bosom, and just shook her head in refusal. This tug of war was probably less than usual, since Carlos had given them the cash for the hormones, and they were not fighting for their own money. Back home, we had weighed this decision carefully. Giving money in documentaries is normally against the rules, in the sense that paying subjects to do or to say things does alter the reality the film is trying to capture. However there are moments when in order to access certain scenes within a reasonable frame of time, the filmmaker might have to fund them. Gigi and Jennifer definitively didn't have the money to buy hormones at this point and even if they had, they would have probably spent it on crack before reaching the old woman in the pharmacy. So we had decided to fund the hormones.

Gigi and Jennifer finally settled with the old woman and stomped out of the pharmacy triumphant but apologetic about having to have paid $65 instead of the traditional $50. Jorge had asked them if they didn't need a prescription for this type of medication.

'Sure you do. If they get the old woman she goes to prison,' said Gigi.

They started shooting when they returned to *The Salt Mines*. Carlos had switched on the camera, while Gigi ran from the gate of the enclosure toward the trucks screaming hoarsely: 'Sara, Sara, we got the hormones! Come on out!'

Surprisingly, the only other person in the enclosure that day was Sara. She crawled out of one of the trucks, her face tinged with the greenish hue of a terrible hangover. It had already started to snow and the light in the shots was a dull charcoal color. Sara sat on a crate crouching over to control her shivering. She didn't even talk or look at the camera that day. But she wouldn't miss the hormones. Gigi had taken out syringes and after giving one to Jennifer she had pierced her needle into one of the hormone vials and was pulling with the syringe to uptake the liquid. Impatiently, she flicked it with her nails to make it descend.

'It's too cold,' said Jennifer, 'The stuff is frozen.'

While they worked breathlessly to warm up the thick gel-like liquid, Carlos asked them why they took hormones.

'How else would we grow breasts and have smooth skin?' answered Gigi totally engrossed in her syringe. 'It's the only way to look like a woman. What else?'

Jennifer's syringe was ready. Holding it in her mouth she unzipped her pants and pulled them down just below the round of the buttocks. Carlos zoomed into a close-up shot while she slapped the frozen surface of her glut a few times and then took the syringe from her lips and stuck the needle into the flesh. The thick hormone gel was too cold to shoot smoothly into the flesh.

'Push hard, mami, just keep pushing,' cheered Gigi and passed one of the syringes to Sara who was still in a sullen mood, shivering on her crate.

Then Gigi turned to the camera. 'Okay, here I go. I'm ready to pull down my pants and shoot up.'

She had already lowered her jeans low enough to expose her butt and with a quick gesture she stabbed her rear end with the syringe. The camera travelled up to her face as her eyes fixated into a frozen stare with dilated pupils. After she injected the content of the syringe, she pulled it out and tossed it over her shoulder towards a pile of garbage lying behind her.

'What were you thinking while you were watching all of this?' I asked Jorge after they ended their account of the shoot.

He grimaced, 'I didn't think anything. I was so disgusted—beyond disgusted, there's just no words…'

I wanted to know his opinion so I could contrast it with my increasing obsession with *The Salt Mines*. I had come to understand that I was really overdoing my involvement with the project. It was all I thought about most of the day. How to film as much as possible before the scene disappeared, how to string together the sequence of events, how to film scenes better. It had become like an addiction, a torturing obsession. Even Carlos was beginning to make comments to the effect of letting go a bit. That night when Jorge left, he said, 'I don't know how many more shoots like this I can take. I think I need a vacation from *The Salt Mines*.'

But I wasn't ready to go anywhere yet.

I t took me about two weeks to recover completely from my strange sickness. When I felt I could leave the apartment, I asked Carlos if we could go down to *The Salt Mines* to follow up on the situation there. It was a few days before Christmas day. It was a cold, clear day and the afternoon light bounced golden rays off the yellow taxi's front window. As we stepped out by the pier and headed towards the compound, we immediately saw there was unusual activity across the entry gate. A caterpillar crane was scooping up the gray salt under the corrugated metal roof and piling it on top of another truck. The salt was getting relocated somewhere else even though snowstorms hadn't even started in the city. We walked by without any interference from the working men. We walked around the trucks for a while. Nobody seemed to be around. I could sense how a deep change was taking place here, but I couldn't put my finger on it.

We went up to Gigi's truck—by now we had learned to distinguish it from the others. I knocked on the metal body close to what I knew was the entrance to her abode.

'Gigi?'

'Who the hell's there?' I heard her gruff voice from the inside.

'Gigi, it's us.'

'Geez, I thought I'd never see you again. Haven't seen you for so long!'

She brought up her face towards the crevice she used to go in and out of the truck, and the orange sun fell on her sleepy eyes and her grayish, tired face.

'I know, I've been sick for weeks,' I told her.

'So have I,' her voice was hoarse and wheezy.

She asked us to wait for a few moments while she got herself together and we heard some fabric and paper rustling noises inside the truck as if she was moving things around. Then she reappeared and started wriggling out of the truck, legs first, then hips and trunk. She moved sluggishly as if it were a big effort. When she was finally out, she coughed and smiled at us weakly. She looked thinner than I remembered her from the last time.

'I lost my voice a couple of days ago. It's been so cold!' She sat on the steps that lead to the driver's seat, hugging her chest. I noticed she wasn't wearing her leather jacket, just an old pea coat and a scarf around her neck.

'Where's Edwin?' I asked.

'Edwin? He got arrested,' she said heavily, and then added forcing a laugh, 'Silly little crook, he got caught again breaking into a car.' Another bout of coughing followed.

When she sobered up, she said, 'Once more, I'm all alone'

We asked her about everyone else. There was no one left in *The Salt Mines* but her. Giovanna had shacked up with a guy, and Sara had managed to get enough money to stay at a hotel called The Terminal.

'What about Ruben?' I asked her.

'Ruben found out he was HIV positive and was taken into Covenant House. They're taking care of him there. He looked real bad in the last few days, sick and skinny.'

She got up and staggered around.

'I'm the last man standing,' she said with a smirk.

She started walking towards the pier taking in the surroundings with the emotion of someone who is walking the earth for the last time. We followed her with the camera.

When she got to the far end of the gray salt mountain, she turned to the camera and said.

'They're going to build a gate here, a huge electronic gate. It'll be impossible to jump it. Now it will be real trespassing, now it will be prison.'

'What will you do?' asked Carlos.

'I want to go back to Puerto Rico, but I need to wait for Edwin to be released. Meantime, I'll have to go back to the street or to the subway. I'm back at square one.'

Then she turned to the camera and pointing toward the salt mountain she said, 'Look, that's where I slept when I first arrived.'

I saw Carlos pan from her face to the darkened summit of the salt mountain.

We heard voices in the distance and saw that a group of Sanitation Department workers clad in green and yellow had entered the truck area and were conducting what looked like some sort of a reconnaissance operation. We had to move on. We asked Gigi to come along with us. The three of us walked through the gate away from the salt mine and the trucks and crossed the 11th Avenue highway, into the Meatpacking District's dark streets. We stopped at the bagel shop on the corner of 14th Street and 9th Avenue. It was a round the clock small shop where they served bagels and coffee under bright fluorescent lights. We ordered egg and cheese bagels and coffee for three. Gigi didn't want to eat inside the shop because she said they knew her and had recently kicked her out. We didn't ask about the details. We just stood with her at the corner and ate our bagels trying not to spill our coffees while we watched the camera and equipment bag at our feet.

Gigi ate quickly and hungrily and as the warm food entered her body I could see her spirit coming back.

When she was done, she said, 'I have to go meet someone,' and took off.

I looked at her as she walked down the avenue with long strides and head held high cutting through the night chill that was descending upon the city. I knew she wasn't going to meet anyone in particular. We had given her just enough fuel to go down to the meat market to hustle and buy herself some crack.

The Salt Mines was shut down with a tall high-tech electronic gate. The Sanitation Department also cleaned up the garbage inside and removed most of the trucks. *The Salt Mines* as we knew it changed very quickly over the next couple of months. I used to go down to the area in the hope I would meet Gigi or Sara and would always walk across the highway towards the enclosure in case some of them might still be hanging around. But the dead of winter had set in and the whole area seemed deserted.

The Educational Video Center classes had also ended, so I was out of a job again. I had lots of time on my hands and six hours of footage from *The Salt Mines*. Six hours! It seemed unreal that we had ended up with only six hours of shot material when in my mind the experience had felt at least months long. But that's another bitter truth about documentary making: even under the best circumstances you only manage to capture a small percentage of the reality you are trying to depict. 10% is already optimal. This explains the documentary producer's angst. No matter how hard you try you can only manage to apprehend so much of reality.

But even within those parameters six hours was ridiculously minimal. Most documentaries work with at least 20:1 ratios, meaning you shoot 20 hours of material to end up with a one hour piece. 6:1 was absurd, but nothing is impossible for the determined filmmaker. There are always ways around the insurmountable.

Another limitation was money. One of the difficulties of film and documentary making is funding. Even if you are willing to work for free, there are always huge costs in materials, equipment, tape transfers, transportation and the whole gamut of different items that make up for those incredibly colossal film budgets. But as I said before, nothing is impossible for a filmmaker on a mission.

I set off to work with what we had: six hours of footage and a secondhand 3/4 inch linear editing system in our walk-in closet. The only urgent expense for now was the tape transfer money, since master tapes could not be used for editing and had to be copied into work tapes. Carlos had just acquired his first credit card for charging traveling expenses on camera jobs, so we put the tape transfers on his card.

We carried the twenty some original tapes in backpacks to Rafik on Broadway and 11th Street. The backpacks were very heavy so we had to take a cab. Every minute of the trip I was afraid something might happen to the tapes: we could get into an accident, we could be mugged, all hell might break loose in the form of an end-of-the-world solar storm or a universal flood, and we would lose our six to one ratio of *The Salt Mines*. The thought of it was unbearable. Even after the taxi left us on Broadway, right in front of Rafik, I thought of all the possible mishaps that could befall us crossing the pavement towards the building and climbing up the legendary extra tall and steep wooden staircase that lead to the actual office of Rafik Film and Videotape, Co. And although everything was fine, and we delivered the tapes without complications, it felt as if I was consigning a baby into foreign hands. I ached until we got them back with duplicates a week later.

I started to edit immediately and struggled for hours on end with the material. I had been well trained as an editor, so my editing skills were strong. But the challenge was not just to edit but to put this material together in a way that would capture all the emotion I had felt while shooting in *The Salt Mines*.

I came up with a 60-minute rough cut that looked very rough, meaning unfinished, and I set about showing it to some colleagues to get opinions on how to polish it. Showing rough cuts is a tricky business. You have to select your viewers very well so as not to waste time, or get sidetracked with opinions that won't serve your final product. Ideally, you should get a few experienced editors and producers, and then contrast their opinions with a couple of perceptive movie goers. I had been present in many rough cut screenings so I was familiar with their dynamics. However, when I started showing *The Salt Mines'* rough cut, one thing really surprised me screening after screening. Most people reacted so strongly to the material that the discussion about technicalities or structure in the editing was always relegated to a secondary order. Everyone wanted to know more about the Salt people, their hows and their whys. The film seemed to open and unquenchable thirst for more information, for endless discussions, for all kinds of personal processing and reactions.

One of my editor friends went as far as to say, 'You know, it doesn't really matter how you edit this—the material is so striking that it's going to carry the story by itself anyway.'

I was upset by this comment, taking it as a negative critique towards my editing skills. And of course, film or video material, no matter how amazing or impressive, needs to be well edited in order to be transmitted to an audience. But it was telling of one unavoidable fact: the reality of *The Salt Mines* took everyone by storm in the same way it had taken me, even when sitting in a tiny, cluttered, walk-in-closet editing room.

Finally, I arrived at a final cut. It was 47 minutes long, a very unorthodox length, but the length I felt the material dictated. Throughout the weeks of working the material over and over, I had ample time to realize all the things I could have shot but didn't, all the things I could have asked but didn't, all the details I missed, all the scenes I could have set up. The editing room is a bitter sweet experience for the director at best. And the resulting 47 minutes of *The Salt Mines* were just about 3% of the reality I had lived through, with my inexperience as a producer director factored into it. But it was still an awesome film. Carlos, who had also trained as an editor, but had spent all this time bringing in the money while I edited, thought so, too. We would sit in the closet editing room watching it over and over. We couldn't believe what we had made together.

Before we locked it into the fine cut, there was one more thing I wanted to do. Show it to the people from *The Salt Mines* and get their go ahead. Showing rough cuts to documentary subjects is not an obligation of the filmmaker, but it is a gesture towards the people who have shared their stories and donated their time. But in the case of *The Salt Mines* I felt it was essential since so much of the material was revealing of sensitive topics, such as sexual identity, prostitution, and drugs. I wanted the main characters of the film to feel comfortable with their disclosure, although it made me nervous to think that they might be offended and ask me to remove scenes or parts of interviews.

There was another problem. We had not obtained any release forms from any of them, or any other written statement in which they agreed to be filmed by us, and the final product to be cut and distributed in any way we thought fit. I knew that releases are essential if a film is going to be shown publicly. They are the basic protection against getting sued by documentary subjects who might be unhappy about how they are portrayed in the final piece. Some of my filmmaker friends had admonished me that if releases are not obtained previously, many subjects will retract from their initial enthusiasm to be filmed and then refuse to sign anything later. I had thought about this many times, but I had been afraid of compromising my friendship with the Salt People by bringing up paperwork suggestive of business and money. I had been afraid of having them ask us for money or refuse to talk openly about certain topics. So I had never brought out the release forms, although I always carried them in the production bag. Now my mistake had come back to haunt me.

This was another powerful reason to start actively looking for Gigi and Sara. I went down to the Meatpacking District in the evenings and talked to every drag queen I encountered. But I soon realized that the population in the meat district was even more changing and elusive than that in *The Salt Mines*. Every week there seemed to be a new batch of young male hustlers and drag queens, and it was hard to find the same people twice. Even harder to get anyone to give any information. I asked around if anyone knew where else there might be groups of homeless transvestites staying, but no one knew anything. Or they didn't want to say.

One day I decided to go to the Terminal Hotel, since Gigi had told me on the last shoot that Sara frequently stayed there. The Terminal Hotel was an old decrepit building at the end of 23rd Street, close to the highway, that had been historically a cheap hotel for marine merchants and other transients, and now posed as a welfare hotel. The entrance hall was extremely narrow and its gray walls thickly swollen with innumerable coats of cheap paint. I was surprised to see that the reception desk was walled in with thick glass or plastic panels, the kind you find in down and out neighborhood liquor stores. The man behind this bullet–or other violence-proof–device was a stocky older man with close shaved gray hair and an impervious face with thick vertical folds of skin around his cheeks and mouth.

'Umm, I'm looking for someone who might be staying here,' I mumbled, suddenly at a loss of words for describing Sara. The man's absent eyes roamed over my face suspiciously.

'Err, her name is Sara, she is a—,' This was ridiculous! Why hadn't I carefully thought before how I would word all this?

Meanwhile a group of people were walking down the hall towards the door. Two big beefy men and a scrawny woman with red hair and very high heels brushed past the reception desk. One of the men nodded at the receptionist and gave me a strange look.

I swallowed and resumed my effort.

'She is a transvestite,' I finally said. 'I really need to find her.'

'Sorry, we don't give out names of residents,' he replied businesslike.

'Please. I *really* need to find her.'

'Look, I don't know anyone by that name or description,' he said dismissively, and pretended to go back to some paperwork on the desk.

I stood for a moment without knowing what to do. Then I said, 'Would you at least let me leave a note just in case you come across her?'

Before he could say anything I took out a note book and quickly scribbled, *Sara, I need to see you urgently*, followed by my telephone number. I slipped the note towards the man under the narrow window slot on the counter. He ignored me for a moment and then took it with an imperceptible sigh.

'Thank you!' I said and walked out of the door into the street.

I knew he was probably going to throw it into the waste paper basket, or at least forget it under his large pile of paperwork. The odds of Sara getting my note were practically nonexistent. It was like putting a message inside a bottle and throwing it into the immensity of the ocean.

Looking for Gigi in the subway was even more despairing. Many homeless people stayed in subways at night, sleeping on benches or even just in corners. Many subway exits around the Chelsea and 14th Street area were used as temporary shelters, and it was not uncommon to find piles of old clothes and bags in corners reeking of

urine and putrid garbage. The *cardboard mattress* was also a staple
item. Homeless people used large pieces of cardboard to lie on at night
and then piled them up in the morning together with other belongings. The situation with the homeless in the subway was as transient as
that in the street, for subway workers united efforts with police to push
people out of spaces and keep them on the move.

At the time Carlos worked as a cameraman with a reporter who was
doing a news documentary on people who were staying in old abandoned train tracks under Grand Central Station. Apparently there were
up to six layers of subway tracks inhabited by a whole population of
homeless, a catacomb city with innumerable passageways connected
with each other like a labyrinth. The news reporter was following a
young girl who was staying down there with her pimp boyfriend. They
entered the tunnels through a ventilation grid inside the station and
descended in pitch darkness through rusty stairs, sets of metal planks
and catwalks until they came to a ridge where the girl was sleeping
inside a heap of blankets. Carlos was blown away by the experience.

Then there was the whole legend of the underground population
living in the Upper West Side, what came to be called the *Mole People*
in Jennifer Toth's book a few years later. Homeless settlements in New
York at the time were whole cities within a city, an unmapped world of
transient urban tribes surviving in a parallel reality.

S pring came and I was ready to lock the project, having given up
on finding anyone.

Then suddenly one morning I was walking up Eighth Avenue

with heavy grocery bags on each hand when I saw two familiar faces walking towards me.

'Gigi! Sara! I don't believe this!'

'Well, look who's finally showing up!'

They kissed me on both cheeks like old girlfriends.

'Where have you been hiding all these months?'

'Me, hiding?' I laughed. It felt good to see them again. They were dressed in the low key girlie attires they usually wore during the day. Gigi wore jeans and a short jacket over a cotton shirt, and Sara wore a knee-length skirt with shabby flat pumps with no stockings. They wore no makeup and Sara's hair was tied back in a ponytail.

'I finished the film,' I said.

'Oh, my God!' said Sara, 'I knew you would end up making us famous!'

'I want you to see it before—'

'Before you send it to Hollywood?' interrupted Sara, 'Sure, I'm game. LET'S GO!'

So we walked together towards my apartment on 21st Street while they chatted animatedly about their comings and goings of the last few months, although I didn't get any clear sense of where they had been or what they had done during the whole time.

When we arrived at the building door and I was about to put the key in the lock, I saw the landlord coming towards down the hall. His name was Mr. Carr and he had recently bought the building and was trying to get rid of the old tenants so he could raise the rents. I had had a few rifts with him about it and we were not on the best of terms. He raised his bushy eyebrows in shocked disapproval at the friends I was bringing into the building as he passed us by. For the first time, I realized I was meeting the Salt People on my turf, *out there in society*, as

Gigi would put it, and that they stood out distinctly as outcasts. But Sara's response was to bat her eyelids at him in seductive jest. Mr. Carr blushed deeply and left the building hurriedly.

Once in the apartment, they oohed and aahed at everything, walking into the different rooms, Sara very forthrightly and Gigi a bit more shyly. I set the grocery bags on the kitchen table and said, 'Let's watch the film.'

'Okay,' said Gigi.

I took them into the closet editing room bringing in extra chairs to place in front of the editing system. While I was setting up the equipment, Sara was going through the clothes that hung bulgingly on the rack opposite the editing system.

'Oh, this is cute. AND LOOK AT THIS!'

'Sara, how could you be so RUDE,' admonished Gigi, 'She asked us to watch the film, NOT to look at her clothes.'

'All right, don't get so worked up about it,' said Sara sitting down.

'Don't worry, I have some clothes for you. But first, let's watch the film.'

I hit the play button and stood up behind them while they watched the full 47 minutes. I was very nervous, particularly when certain scenes or parts of interviews came up. But Gigi and Sara laughed at most scenes, and really hard at the fight scene which I had feared Gigi would be upset about. Then they became emotional at others. I saw Gigi quietly shedding a few tears when she heard herself talk about her mother.

'What do you think? Is it all right with you?' I asked them when it was over.

'It's great' they said, and I could tell they had enjoyed it.

Carlos walked into the apartment.

'Hey guys! What a surprise!' he greeted. They relapsed into the flirtatious behavior they always displayed when there was a male around.

After they had settled down from their exuberant greetings, I took the occasion to say, 'If you like the film, would you give us written permission to show it around?'

'Of course!' said Sara, 'Bring on any papers, I'll sign.'

And they both signed the releases I had carried countless times in our equipment when we went shooting in *The Salt Mines.*

Carlos had brought a large takeout of Cuban food from restaurant down the block, so we set the kitchen table and began to eat. Our kitchen was small, and the table was a fairly large butcher's block that took up most of the room, but that made it even cozier when friends huddled around the packed table at dinner parties. Gigi and Sara ate hungrily enjoying every morsel. I asked them where they had stayed over in the winter months and they told me they had taken shelter in some abandoned elevated tracks that run from 14th to 34th Street, where it was very cold because there were very few covered shelter spaces, but private and hassle free because police or city workers hardly ever went there. This was the first time I heard about the High Line, an old system of freight transport between factories and warehouses that had been built in the 1930s and now was totally abandoned. But for Gigi and Sara, nothing could be compared with *The Salt Mines,* because on the elevated tracks they said, besides being much colder, the surrounding district was not optimal for hustling. 34th Street by 11th Avenue was a *real* women's prostitution area protected by very aggressive pimps who didn't want drag competition.

When we finished eating I started clearing the table but Sara jumped out of her seat and said, 'Please, please let me wash the dishes. I just LOVE running water,' and running to the sink she turned on the faucet full force and started doing the dishes noisily while she splashed as much water around as she could. Every now and then, she would turn towards the table to join in on the conversation but left the still faucet running behind her. I wanted to ask her to be mindful of the amount of water she was wasting, but I didn't say anything because I could see she was relishing the whole experience.

I brought out a bag of clothes that my friend Idoia had given me a few weeks before. There was nothing spectacular in it, just old T-shirts and used dance leggings and leg warmers. But everything Idoia owned was always beautiful, even if it had been worn to the bone. As soon as I spread the things on the table, I saw Gigi's eyes glitter. Sara darted over instantly and I took the opportunity to turn off the water. They looked admiringly at every piece.

'All these are for us?' Sara asked.

'Yes, just make sure you share them,' I said and Gigi laughed.

'Do you mind if I use your bathroom to change?' asked Sara.

There was a larger question within the question. I looked at them and saw once more how dirty they were, their skin, their hair and of course, the clothes they were wearing. I looked at Carlos who was standing at the door observing the whole scene. The moment we locked eyes I knew he was thinking exactly the same thing. He didn't even have to nod to agree.

I said, 'Don't you want to have a shower before you put on the new clothes?'

Sara looked at me for a second in disbelief. 'Sure! Is that possible?'

We set them up with towels and shampoo in our tiny bathroom with its ancient porcelain bathtub standing on tiny lion feet. Each of them took a lengthy shower and emerged humid and glowing in their new outfit. We put their discarded clothes into a plastic bag to throw into the garbage. Carlos had made coffee, but they had no time to sit again at the table and drink it leisurely. They sipped it standing and I knew they were impatient to get back to the street. We had given them again all they needed for a great evening at the meat market.

The doorbell rang and Jorge, who had agreed to deliver some paperwork to Carlos, was on his way up. Gigi and Sara brightened up even more at the sight of Jorge. Suddenly there was a boisterous crowd in our narrow hallway.

'Oh, here's my fellow countryman lawyer,' said Gigi bashfully.

'How come you never introduce THESE MEN FRIENDS to me?' said Sara turning towards me in a dramatical gesture.

When they left, Jorge sat in the kitchen and we made more coffee.

When he saw the pile of wet towels I was putting in a laundry bag, he said, 'Did you really let them shower in your bathroom? You better make sure you spray Clorox thoroughly all over.'

My first thought was that our good friend Jorge had an extreme pathological fear of germs, but on second thought I realized he might have a point. Shouldn't I have been more cautious? Maybe. But in a way, who can deny a shower to someone who hasn't washed in days or weeks? It felt like refusing food to a hungry person.

Jorge went on. He was genuinely concerned about our safety.

'Aren't you afraid they will steal from you if you bring them up here?' he asked.

The thought had never crossed my mind. Other than our equipment, we had nothing of value in the apartment. And for the first time in all these months, I considered that no one in *The Salt Mines* had ever taken anything from us, asked us for money or for anything else for that matter.

After we locked the picture and finished the sound editing, we needed to go onto the next phase which was called a fine cut. It meant going to a professional post-production house and having them transfer everything into a larger format, normally 1" videotape, and edit everything all over again on huge editing systems that took up whole rooms. When going to fine cut sessions, everything had to be finalized and all sound tracks, music and subtitles, if any, had to be perfectly ready and organized. There could be no mistakes at fine cuts because it was a point of no return in the project, unless you could afford to pay for it all over again. Fine cut sessions were very expensive, in the range of $250 to $1000 per edited minute, depending on the complexity of the project. A real fortune in those days.

We had no way of getting hold of a sum like that. We had reached a stalemate point in the project.

However, there is a saying in the film world that sometimes it is the *film that chooses you and not the other way around*. What this means is that the producer or director can just become pawns in the making of a project that has its own reasons to be shot, finished and poured into the culture's collective consciousness. In such cases the film, or the invisible powers that move it along, seem to mysteriously resolve problems and surmount obstacles in order to fulfill its completion. This saying suddenly made sense to me when, out of the blue, a solution to the funding problem landed on my lap.

I had an Argentinian friend called Oswaldo who was a painter, but more than anything was a patron of the arts. He had recently taken on an old abandoned gas station on 2nd Street and Avenue B and converted it into a funky bar and performance space. The bar was in the same small room the gas station office had been in, and the adjacent performance space was the old garage where cars got fixed. The floor was still the old grease dirty concrete floor, and the whole structure was heated up by a huge industrial blower that had to be turned off during performances and band concerts because of its unbearable noise. Most of the drinking and socializing took place outside around the old gas pumps. But this casual industrial recycling style was the fad of the day, and the Gas Station Cafe became a downtown cutting edge space where local artists could present their work.

Oswaldo knew about *The Salt Mines* and had always been interested in the project, so he called me one day to ask me if I would be interested in applying for film finishing funds. I had no idea such possibilities existed but I accepted and started working immediately with him and his grant-writer, Mark, a poet who worked as an accountant during the day.

We wrote a grant to NYSCA, or the New York State Council on the Arts, requesting money to finish *The Salt Mines* and to my surprise, we were awarded $15,000 and made Fellows of the Council. Having worked all this time with no money at all, this was a fortune to us. We could pay for a fine cut and even a musician to compose for the film. Oswaldo introduced us to an experimental musician who was part of the Downtown music scene and was willing to compose music for *The Salt Mines*. His name was Elliot Sharp.

I first saw Elliot performing at the Gas Station Cafe. He was playing a solo piece on a saxophone. A harsh red light silhouetted his slim wiry body against the corrugated metal of the Cafe's gate. His head was completely shaved and his face seemed carved out of a rock, with large eyes, a huge nose and thick lips that wrapped powerfully around the saxo's mouthpiece. He held the instrument with such intensity that it seemed they were fused together. There was a staggering quality in the notes that blew out of his glittering saxo. A harsh jagged bleating of dissonant notes in search for new sounds. But running underneath, there was a deep sense of song that pulsated into your body and electrified the whole room.

I was very taken by his performance. Later at the bar, when Oswaldo introduced me to Elliot what struck me most was the deep calm in his eyes. I guess I had expected him to be full of angst after listening to him play. But he was a shy, bashful guy, soft spoken and attentive. We talked about his music and I told him about the Salt People. Oswaldo stood behind the bar listening intently to our conversation while he sold beers and other drinks to customers. In order to celebrate the deal that was very quickly coming together between us, he presented us with the special drink of the house: the Gas Station Cocktail, an explosive blend of watermelon, vodka and mint leaves that he mixed noisily behind the bar in a home blender. It was strong and delicious.

'Isn't he awesome?' asked Oswaldo after Elliot left, 'Do you know he invents musical instruments? He is perfect for the project.' There was a huge grin on his face, the kind he spread across his face when he talked about the talent he was digging out of the East Village for performances in his cafe.

I walked away from the Gas Station Cafe in total exhilaration that night. The idea of having someone as powerful as Elliot add to the project, his saxophone playing over the frozen old trucks, over the tough and tender faces of the drag queens, was making my head reel. I was beginning to get a taste of what it means to work in a collective effort towards a project: each artists brings a new enhancement to the piece, magnifying the beauty and power of its message. A new dimension, impossible to achieve individually.

The Salt Mines was a great success. We premiered at the Gas Station Cafe in order to honor the unbending support he had received from Oswaldo and his non-profit corporation. But almost immediately we started getting requests to show it in other art spaces and festivals. The first festival where it won the prize of Best Video Documentary was the National Latino Film and Video Festival in New York in 1991. Other prizes followed immediately in New Jersey, San Antonio, and even in Havana, Cuba, where it was given a *Premio Coral*, as Best Video on a Latin American theme by a non-Latin American Filmmaker.

After those first festivals, the distribution of *The Salt Mines* took off by itself. We were constantly getting invitations and requests to show it in Gay and Lesbian festivals, in museums, performance spaces, libraries, and local and national public and television programs. It got press reviews all over the place and started to get distributed into college and library collections. It traveled extensively around the United States and abroad.

*The Salt Mines* seemed to have soared into life of its own. It was no longer in our hands.

Although *The Salt Mines* was finished and well on its way into the world, I hadn't given up on finding the rest of the Salt People to show them the finished documentary and ask them to sign release forms. Particularly Giovanna, who was one of the main subjects together with Gigi and Sara. But she proved to be impossible to find. The last time I had seen Gigi, she had told me that Giovanna had a sister and a mother who lived in the Bronx and who, despite everything, accepted her as she was and always helped her and took her back whenever she knocked on their door. So Giovanna was not permanently homeless, she had a definite home base, and only spent a few weeks on the street when she got very heavily into crack, or other drugs. A family made all the difference in the world.

Signed releases were not neccessary any more, though. When approached by Channel 13 for broadcast we were told that in cases like these the only prerequisite was the purchase of a reasonably priced insurance policy that would cover any suits coming from disgruntled subjects. I was surprised at the existence of such a simple solution, after having tormented myself to no end on this issue.

'*Suuure*, like that would fly if the subjects were white and system-savvy with deep pockets!' said my friend Lisa when I told her. Lisa was also in the documentary world, and very sensitive towards social issues.

Her comment came as a lash. It was true. What power would any of the Salt People have to protest against the public exposure of their lives? And anyway, what was their gain in the whole bargain? Besides the attention, a few shared bagels and cups of coffee, and the healing effect of telling your story, what else? We hadn't paid them any money for their time or collaboration. This is not done in documentary making. Of course, no one had paid us either; it had been a self-funded independent project. It wouldn't bring in huge revenues either, but at least we were building on our career as filmmakers. But what were they getting in the deal?

A year or so after the broadcasting of *The Salt Mines* on Channel 13's national program, Independent Focus, I was walking on 14th Street one afternoon when I saw a group of drag queens talking animatedly on the corner of 9th Avenue. One of them looked very much like Ruben, although very changed. It wasn't just the shoulder length blonde hair and the heavy makeup that made up for the transformation. It was a more like a blooming, the kind you see in girls when they start becoming women. The way his features had opened up and softened, the way his body had taken on graceful postures. He was wearing a silky green dress under a short cream jacket and high heel shoes. His legs were muscular but shapely under white shimmering tights, and he gestured delicately with his hands as he spoke leaning slightly against a street lamp post. The other two were listening intently. It looked like an intimate conversation.

I went up to them. 'Ruben?' I asked tentatively.

He turned his eyes towards me. This was definitely not a *he* anymore, but a *she*. There was a dreamy smile that started in her brown eyes and followed down the high cheek bones to the corner of her large plump lips. The soft pupils searched mine for a moment before a spark of recognition lit up her whole face.

'Oh my God! I can't believe this!' and turning around to her friends she said, 'This is the woman filmmaker I've told you so much about. Isn't she lovely?'

'Ruben, I finished the film. It's showing all over the place.'

'It's not Ruben anymore, it's Ruby,' she said, blushing slightly. 'I know the film has been on TV and all,' she added after a moment with an excited look on her face. 'I haven't seen it, but I've been told it's *the* best!'

'I can show it to you whenever you want.'

'Oh, but you know what happened?' her tone changed suddenly and her eyes darkened.

'What?' I asked, feeling a vague sense of anxiety. I thought she was going to give me a piece of bad news concerning someone from *The Salt Mines*.

Ruben took a short step towards me and lowered her voice slightly.

'You know when it went on TV? My family saw it and that's how they found out I had HIV,' she said and looked at me directly in the eye. There was no recrimination or bitterness in her gaze. There was only a sweet sadness in the depth of her eyes. My heart began to race as I started to take in the implications of what she had just told me.

'Oh no, no!' I mumbled, 'Ruby, I am so sorry—I never…'

Ruby laid a hand on my arm and pressed it slightly. I felt the warmth of her skin against mine. 'That's how things are. I wish they hadn't learnt about it that way, but we can't change it now,' she said soothingly, and her sweetness felt like a knife slicing through my chest.

'We need to be on our way now, but I'll see you around,' she said and she let go of my arm, smiling.

'Ruby, I can show you the film whenever you want. My apartment is right around the corner. Let me give you…' I was quickly scribbling my telephone number on a piece of paper. She took it and folding it neatly, put in in her handbag. We looked at each other for a moment. We both knew she would never call on me. She was too shy or too afraid to see the film.

She turned around to her friends, 'OK girls, let's go!' and then back at me, 'It has been so lovely to see you!' and she kissed me delicately on both cheeks while her friends looked on eagerly.

My eyes followed them as they swayed their hips down the street, flicking their hair and pouting their lips at male passersby. The image of Ruben-Ruby's green dress swiveling around her body as she disappeared into the crowd stayed in my mind.

I walked back home with a heavy heart. Carlos was away for the day on a shoot. I sat around for a while feeling an unbearable weight in my chest and tightness in the throat. After a while, feeling terribly restless, I tried to find some chore to keep my mind engaged somewhere else. But to no avail. Ruben's words kept going around in my mind. How could I not have thought about the implications of stating such a private medical condition in a documentary that that we intended to screen publicly, and maybe even broadcast nationally? Moreover, information about a condition such as AIDS, a condition that provoked all kinds of panic stricken reactions, since it was perceived as the leprosy of the day. What could I have been thinking? It hadn't even crossed my mind, and truth be told, nobody who had screened the film had ever mentioned anything about it. The memory of the sweetness with which Ruben had told me, his sad, forgiving eyes, felt like a poison trickling into my bloodstream with each painful heartbeat. It would have been easier to have been screamed at. But Ruben had stated facts with such simplicity, his face open with the innocence with which victims stare out of horror pits and torture chambers. She had even spared me the harrowing details of the drama it must have meant for her and her family.

I thought about Truman Capote and his controversial *In Cold Blood*, and how he had built up his literary success by exposing the criminal pattern of a poor wretch. I thought about the deep consequences and the responsibility of depicting people's lives. There was no doubt in my mind that the closing of *The Salt Mines* had, if nothing else, been accelerated by our filming. I had also seen with my own eyes how feeding and clothing the Salt People had real and immediate consequences, supporting their prostitution and drug habits. And now, I had just found out about the most distressing outcome of all, the ravaging of an individual and his family's privacy. I wondered if Truman Capote had considered the potential repercussion of his work, or if he had just been driven by artistic ambition. I certainly had been driven by my producer ambition. I had pushed relentlessly to film every detail of *The Salt Mines* and interviewed to probe deep into its people's hearts and minds. In my craze, I had been convinced that the world needed to have a close look at this reality to better understand the predicament of its inhabitants. But now I was wondering how all this information was going to benefit anyone at all.

That night, I went to bed completely crushed.


In February 1991 we had been invited to screen *The Salt Mines* at the Guadalupe Cinefestival in San Antonio, Texas. They were flying us down so we could be present at the screening and then talk about the film and take questions from the audience. I was very much looking forward to this event and to the trip with Carlos. *The Salt Mines* had been selected by many film festivals but very few of them ever had the resources to pay filmmakers' travel and hotel expenses.

The day before our trip, I was at home packing and putting together materials for the talk when the doorbell rang. I pushed the open-door button on the intercom system thinking it was the laundry delivery I had been expecting. But when I opened the apartment door, I was surprised to see Sara.

'Sara! Such a long time!'

'Is this a bad time?'

'Not at all. Come in.'

She walked into the kitchen, took off her coat and sat at the table. She was thinner than I had ever seen her. Her hip and shoulder bones stuck out under her clothes. She had no makeup on and her complexion was grayish around her hollow eyes. She sat hugging her chest.

'How are you, girl?' she said trying to sound cheerful. But I already knew there was something wrong.

'Don't you have a little coffee for me?' The way she said *cafecito* in a drawling Cuban accent spoke of her desperate need for affection.

I started making coffee while I told her about the San Antonio festival and the trip we were taking there. But she was distracted. When I set the coffee mugs on the table and sat opposite her, she stirred sugar into her coffee in silence for a few moments. I watched her short bitten nails with old traces of burgundy nail polish.

Suddenly she said, 'I need to tell you something'

My chest tightened in anticipation of another piece of bad news.

'My mother passed away last month in La Habana,' she said and tears started streaming down her face. I felt my eyes sting as I got pulled into her emotion. I asked her how she had found out about it. She told me she had heard from a neighbor who had a telephone and who would fetch her mother from next door every time she called. The neighbor told her that her mother had come down sick and was taken to the hospital where she died a few hours later. The neighbor didn't have any other medical information. She was a sweet old woman with very little education. Sara didn't have anyone else to call in La Habana to find out more about the death or the burial. For the first time it occurred to me that Sara had had a mother all this time with whom she had kept in contact regularly, even while she lived on the street.

'You have no other family you can contact?'

She shook her head and held her silence for a beat.

'But there's something else. I got tested for HIV. The results were positive.'

My heart shrunk as I watched tears break slowly through her hot swollen eyes. I reached over and touched her hand. It was cold and rough.

'What will you do?' I asked in an attempt to break up the emotion that was growing monstrously thick in the room.

'That's what I came to talk to you about.'

So, the hard part was yet to come. Something inside me stiffened at the thought she might ask me for something. My mind was already scanning wildly for arguments against giving her any money, lodging her in our apartment or fulfilling any other demanding request.

But she only said, 'I wanted to know your opinion about the possibility of going with the church.'

Shame washed over me and drowned my voice for a moment. I couldn't believe the list of arguments that had just run through my mind against all the possible things she might ask me to do or give. I looked around the kitchen for a moment and took in all the things I owned: a table, an old colorful collection of pots and pans, a working cooker and refrigerator, a home with radiators noisily exuding heat this very second, and then at her, so small, clutching her coffee mug, her mouth taut, her eyes sad and strangely serene at the same time.

'The church? You mean Terry's church?' I repeated in a dry whisper.

'Who else will take me?' she asked simply, 'It's my only choice.'

'But there are programs, the gay community is organizing against AIDS, there are people who can help you, I will help you find them, I will make phone calls…' A sort of fever was coming over me, a rush of heated ideas and plans that wanted to scrub away the guilt I was feeling.

'Really, think about it,' she suddenly sobered up and sat straight. 'Who's going to take me? A *cubano* drag queen living on the street. The *americano* gays? They are so ashamed of us. The hospitals? I don't have insurance, I don't even speak English properly.'

I argued with her. There are non-profits that take care of health situations, I said, there are social workers in hospitals and clinics who speak Spanish and are Latino themselves, there are ways into the system, and out of the street and AIDS. But she wouldn't yield.

'I love your enthusiasm,' she laughed at one point, 'You sound more obstinate that a pair of Cuban oxen.' I relaxed some and laughed with her. My impassioned brainstorming wasn't taking us anywhere.

'Seriously, I think the only ones who can help me in my situation are the church people.'

'But what will they want in exchange?'

'That is the problem. The *cositas*–little things–they want are–'

She went on to tell me that Terry had already instructed her about taking her down to Dallas, where their church had a special ministry for transsexuals and their transformation back to men and manly ways. She would have to cut her hair, start dressing like a man again, relearn masculine mannerisms and practice manly chores, and she would have to forget her drag name and be called Ricardo again. In terms of her silicone breasts, since they were just cheap injections shot into the breast tissue, it was doubtful they could remove the substance while she was infected with HIV. He would just have to wear a sort of girdle around the chest under his shirt so they wouldn't show. In exchange for all of this, they would provide accommodation, food and medical care.

'Is that all?' I asked, remembering the story about Veronica that Giovanna and Gigi had told me in *The Salt Mines*. She faltered for a moment while a dark shadow crept into her eyes.

'There's one thing more. I will have to make public confessions during Sunday services in front of the congregation and also, I'll have to help them when they go around evangelizing other drag queens. That's the hardest part.'

'You can't be serious!'

But she was. At least the terms had been laid out candidly. The church would help only if they could revert her to what they thought was the will of the Lord: a eunuch in the service of God. And then use her to indoctrinate others. I thought of the penitent heretic victims of the Spanish Inquisition. I felt fury exploding and burning me inside out. I felt hatred for Terry, who had never returned any calls. I felt hatred for the Dallas ministry and their self-appointed priesthood that purged human beings who didn't fall into their narrow norms and definitions.

Sara poked me.

'Girl, what are you thinking about now? I need you to concentrate and help me make a decision here.'

'Sara, what can I tell you? I detest those guys. They go against everything I believe in,' I said looking away through the kitchen window where an old cherry tree swayed in the breeze heavy with white flowers on its branches. Spring was really early this year.

'But… ?' she asked searching out my eyes with hers.

But. Was it in the end her best, or even her only choice? I cringed at the thought of Sara languishing with AIDS and lost in the labyrinth of Medicare and public city hospitals under the random care of homophobic nurses and social workers, who considered people like her human garbage. One thing about the church was that they found a purpose with drag queens like Sara. And that gave them some value.

I sat dejected. Sara emptied the coffee dregs of her mug.

'So, do you think I should take their offer?'

'All in all, Sara, I think maybe you should. At least until you get better,' I heard myself saying in a metallic voice. It felt like betrayal in the face of unconquerable defeat. I couldn't take on Sara. Even if I had wanted to, it was too great a commitment for someone like me. So, how could I ask anyone else to do it?

'Okay. I really needed to hear your opinion,' said Sara and it was as if a huge weight had lifted from her voice.

'What do you say to another *cafecito*?' she asked. This time, *cafecito* sounded playful and leisurely fun, as if we had been sitting in a cafe in old Habana on a lazy afternoon.

Carlos returned a few hours after Sara left. When I told him the whole story, he was horrified. None of my arguments could convince him that there was any advantage for Sara to turn to the Church. He vowed he would go down to 14th Street the next day to find her, and talk her out of it. And he did go hunting for her a few times, but never found her.

For years I wondered about the amount of controversy that *The Salt Mines* triggered among audiences. We were never done with questions and comments when the Q & A time was over after screenings. Young and old, educated and uneducated, all genders, races and cultural backgrounds—most viewers were challenged. We often stayed over time discussing endless topics with the audience. Years after its release, people called and wrote notes and letters about the film. The project itself went around the world into every Gay and Lesbian festival in the globe. But it wasn't just gay and lesbian audiences who showed interest. Even today, *The Salt Mines* is owned by most Film and Video Department universities and colleges libraries around the United States.

There was something in *The Salt Mines* that touched a deep spot in people, something that disturbed the business-as-usual mode in which most people live their lives. In a way, *The Salt Mines*, with all its squalor, its grime and freezing winds, represented a picture of radical freedom, in the sense that its inhabitants had given up all the things most of us cling to, like security and convention, to pursue life as a raw modality.

Once we were invited to screen *The Salt Mines* at the public library in Port Washington, Long Island. Like in most of these screenings, the library offered only travel expenses and a symbolic stipend for the filmmaker to present the film and then take Q & As. Going out to Long Island on a Thursday evening in December was basically a labor of love. But from the beginning I had been determined to take any possible opportunity to show and discuss the film. When I arrived at the library, I saw there were only about ten people gathered for the screening. Most of them were senior citizens. The curator, a very nice woman, was apologetic about the size of the audience. But I knew how much she must have liked *The Salt Mines* in order to organize a screening out here. We showed the film and then I stood up in front of the group and talked about the Salt People. Coming mostly from New York screenings where audiences are extremely diverse and openly accepting of any cutting-edge story, I suddenly felt insecure in front of an older and more conservative audience. But I was in for a surprise.

I took the first question from an older man sitting in the front row

'I confess I am very impressed at the level of intelligence of these people,' he said, 'I'm ashamed to admit that whenever I see people on the streets, I tend to assume they are mentally disabled.'

I asked him what scene or interview had made the most impression on him.

'There were a few, but the part where–is her name Giovanna?– talked about God, I think was the main one. I guess we all have formulated those kinds of doubts at some point.'

'I think what impressed me most was their courage,' added a little old lady sitting with a friend, 'I can't imagine myself living in such conditions surrounded by all those dangers.'

'In our society, we tend to think that anyone who isn't in the mainstream is worthless,' A younger man in a suit sitting alone at the back of the room said, 'But these people teach us a lesson. We are all slaves to the system.'

All heads turned around to look at him. There was a beat of silence. He was probably in his late forties, well dressed and clean shaven, and looked like he had come straight from his corporate job to the screening.

'Well, I wouldn't go that far,' said another woman. She looked in her sixties, with long hair and colorful clothes, a local ceramic artist, as she would introduce herself to me later. 'They have put themselves in a very difficult position, and it is true that our system has no safety net for anyone who falls below a certain point. But I think they have gone a bit too far.'

'These people have no fear of death,' continued the man in the suit in passionate crescendo, 'They live in total freedom. No mortgage, no bills, no nine to five job. They live one day at a time.'

'But at the cost of a great deal of suffering,' retorted the artist.

'There is also suffering in mainstream lives. And what is much worse, mental and spiritual death.' answered the man in the suit.

This exchange was cut short by the curator sweetly informing it was time to leave because the library was closing. People flooded towards me to make last minute comments or ask questions. I looked around for the man in the suit but he was already gone.

I watched the dark winter night scattered with glittering lights pass me by as I sat in the train on my trip back to the city. I thought of the African professor I had met on one of the first shoots in *The Salt Mines*, and how he had predicted that making a documentary on homelessness would have no impact on the world. *People don't care*, he had said. His words had cast a shadow of doubt that had lingered in my mind for the entire making of *The Salt Mines*. I now held up his despondent words against the deep impact that the discussion at the Port Washington Library had had on me. In the midst of a seemingly suburban conservative community, I had witnessed one of the most passionate and interesting discussions that would ever follow a screening of *The Salt Mines*. These people had been deeply moved by the film. For 47 minutes, they had plunged into an alternative reality that had made them laugh, cry, cringe, fear and share their deeper humanity with a group of characters they would have never encountered in real life. This was the power of documentaries. Pulling us close up to situations we have slim chances of experiencing directly. And through this exposure, shaking up the comfortable patterns we live in, stirring our dead emotions and questioning our prejudices, as we see ourselves reflected in others. Since, at the end of the day, all human experience is universal.

Made in the USA
Lexington, KY
07 March 2014